FEMININE WARRIOR

Your Guide to Intuition and
Feminine Wisdom

Rachel,

Let your path always be
illuminated with love.

xoxo

♡ Deann

Jam-packed with accessible, divine guidance and practical day-to-day strategies, *Feminine Warrior* is the handbook that modern-day millennial women are craving. Deanna's entertaining, candid storytelling and beyond-her-years' insights make each page a delight to read, offering much food for thought and plenty of revelations. Whether you're a seasoned spiritual seeker or just starting to dip your toes in, *Feminine Warrior* is an invitation to go deep while keeping it real and having fun!

~Alice Bracegirdle, CEO and Founder Bellyfit® Enterprises Inc.

Feminine Warrior is a must-read book, full of divine guidance, deep honesty, and the how-to strategies to embody your Feminine gifts and superpowers. I can't wait to share this profound book with all of the women in my life!

~Cheryl Paige, Goddess of Light, Mama, Wife, and Creative

Feminine Warrior is an incredible exploration of the very highest and ultimate potentials that women possess. Through Deanna's poignant writing, women of all walks of life will be awakened to the recognition of their own powers. *Feminine Warrior* is a handbook to discovering our deep truths and a guide to embracing our feminine spirit. It's a book for healing and growth that is engaging, effective, and enlightening. The teachings in this book are a catalyst for walking lightly, but with strength, as a woman in this world.

~Karen Peterson, Owner of Blissed Out Yoga and Fitness Studio

In her storytelling-infused, spiritually aligned, self-help and resource guide, Deanna walks every woman through the journey from uncertain, unaware, and afraid, to Empowered, Awakened, and Embodied as their own *Feminine Warrior.*

~Vanessa Ooms, Intuitive Graphic Designer

Praise for *Feminine Warrior*

Truer words have never been spoken: "We are alive in a time when feminine leadership is a requirement for humanity's evolution." In fact, this is the very reason why we have come into this time and space. We, like Deanna, are here to guide those who are ready for their inward journey to finally release their wounds, rise and BECOME. This book is vulnerable, open, wise, and absolutely pure guidance from the Divine for women everywhere to do just that. There are absolutely no mistakes. You have been guided to this book, to these words, to these tools, to these stories, for every single reason you are alive. Each question asked of you has a profound power and ability to cause a personal inward revolution! Awareness of self, love of self, the courage needed to finally become all that you were born to be can be attained by reading these words and practicing these tools. As Deanna teaches in *Feminine Warrior*, it is the softening into oneself that will be your path to a blissful, abundant awakening. As each of you awakens, so does the world. This book provides the tools to do just that. We wish you a happy journey.
~*The Oracle, as channeled by Sonja Foss*

Reading *Feminine Warrior* by Deanna Deacon felt like a return to my whole self—inside out. It is soulful, pragmatic, and gives one ample opportunity to reflect wholeheartedly on what it truly means to live a life filled with joyful desire. These are tools and wisdom that every human being should have! If you want to learn how to harness both your feminine and masculine energies in life, love, and business, this is THE book for you!
~*Tania Moraes-Vaz, Author, Editor, Founder at Warrior Life Creative Inc., Serial Entrepreneur*

We are in the process of healing generations' worth of trauma and oppression; *Feminine Warrior* is a good conversation starter on how to begin the work of stepping naturally into our embodied feminine energy and healing up by healing in.

~*Leisse Wilcox, Transformational Mindset + Success Coach*

I went from feeling broken, damaged, and not keeping up to reading this book and finding my ROAR. There were so many moments when reading page after page that I screamed out loud, "YES!!!!!!!!" This book breathed new breath into me and gave me, the reader, a true awakening!
Chapter after chapter helped me to dig deep into my own head, but then deeper into my heart and soul. A must-read book for goddesses everywhere!!!

~*Lori Mork, Best-Selling Author of Kiss My Curvy Assets, Fitness and Wellness Coach*

Dear sisters, this book is your call back to your fierce feminine self. It will guide you into activating the power within that you have ignored for too long. It will remind you that you are the embodiment of every strong woman who has walked before you, those of us here walking beside you now, and the women to come. This book is for you if you are ready to step up, show up, and open your heart to the infinite creative power held within your very being. Every page was a huge yes for me and the empowering reminder we all need. I believe every woman on the planet would benefit from reading this book! It's a Goddess guidebook leading you down the path to fully embodying the radiant, Graceful warrior within. I leave this note with the deepest gratitude for Deanna, for writing this book, for having the courage to share her story fiercely, and for all of the important work she is doing during this potent time on our planet. I'm beyond honored to have a little part in this and the opportunity to send my love to Deanna and all sisters whose hands this book lands in. I know this offering will create a huge wave in the collective rising of the fierce feminine.

Thank you, Deanna.

Thank you, sisters.

Together we rise higher.

~Krystal Aranyani

For every woman awakening to her Truth:

I see you;

I feel you;

I'm right here with you.

CONTENTS

FEMININE WARRIOR

Your Guide to Intuition and Feminine Wisdom

DEANNA DEACON

PREFACE

This is how we experience life: through moments in time, deep intro-spection, emotional breakdown, and choosing to rise again, regardless of the situation. We connect most deeply through stories; our ances-tors knew this fact centuries before we did. And in this golden age of social spirituality, it almost feels rebellious . . . it feels rebellious to be who you are. It feels rebellious to show up and share your heart, share your Truth—without a mask, without a façade, without apology.

This book is your rebellion—your rebellion against every time you've felt unsafe in your body, every time you've held your tongue instead of speaking your Truth, every time you've felt judged and isolated from your sisters.

Awaken to your RISE, my love.
Your journey home begins now.

You are a modern woman doing everything you can to "make it" in today's society. You are doing all the things, playing all the roles, all the time. You are a mother, a wife, a best friend, a workout buddy, a soul seeker, a side-business hustler, an Instagram junkie, a nutrition seeker, a lover of the Earth and all things beautiful, but . . . and let's be honest here . . . in real life, it's a bit messy. It's chaotic. It's anything but pretty and put together.

On paper, your life may be what you signed up for—the family, the house, the career, the friends, the life where you are all the things, all the time, but the truth is that there is something missing.

You are unhappy and unsatisfied—complacent even. You feel as though you are drifting through life, at times lacking motivation or fearing change, yet knowing that this current reality can't possibly be it for the rest of your life. There has to be more: more purpose, more intention, and more joy, right? Goals no longer excite you the way they once did. It now feels like you're simply checking off the boxes so you can stay within the rulebooks of society. And not once have you ever paused and asked yourself, "Why do I feel this way?" or "Is this what I truly want?"

This book will stir up fire within—like on that episode of *Friends* when the girls read the book *Be Your Own Windkeeper* and began arguing about stealing each other's wind and lightening bearers. There certainly was inner fire roaring that day, but they directed it at each other. In this book you will learn how to feel that fire within, notice your desire to blame and judge, and step instead into your own innate power.

You've been asking the Universe, Source, God to send you a sign—this is the sign you've been asking for. There are no such things as coincidences, simply Divine synchronicity. You chose to read this book for a reason. You are here to receive the message that is for you, with you, of you.

A love letter to the warrior woman within

Dear Warrior Woman,

We need you to know how valuable you are.
We need you to wake up to the Truth of your being.
We need you to stop hiding behind the conformity of society and instead allow yourself to awaken to the beauty and bounty of who you are.
You are a magnificent, incredible, and beautiful woman.
You were born into a time in humanity that needs your magnificence to be felt, believed, and lived so deeply.

The Conscious Collective has been in cycles of suffering for decades, allowing the pain of the whole to be felt on an individual level. They say we cannot change the actions or outcomes of another person . . . but I believe we can. I have seen it, and I have experienced it.

When a woman embodies her Truth, she rises and allows others to rise with her.
When she finally comes home to the awareness and understanding that she is a life giver, body healer, truth teller, and symbol of the purest form of love, magical shifts take place both for herself and anyone in her energetic orbit.

Warrior Woman, when you rise and stand strong in your Truth, the world aligns with your beliefs, your desires, your values. And within this unveiling of your Truth lies the absolute beauty of your wholeness . . .

When empowered, there is no leadership based in fear, no worry or doubt that you are not good enough.
You are embodied in the simplicity and strength of already being it ALL.
And within you is the absolute power and ability to fulfill humanity's need.
You CAN love yourself; you CAN feel whole; you CAN find your peace. You are on the journey of becoming the world's feminine warrior. This is your path, your homecoming, your celebration of the magical tapestry that your life truly is. This is you.

INTRODUCTION

We are alive in a time when feminine leadership is a requirement for humanity's evolution. There are massive levels of suffering, brokenness, and fear, all because we have been living in an imbalanced state, a wounded state—a wounded and imbalanced masculine and feminine. Now the time has come to awaken to the inherent wisdom and infinite strength of feminine energy that will elevate humanity to a higher frequency of living. You are needed for this rising. You are needed for this evolution. You are needed—in your wholeness, in your fullness, in your you-ness—to be the feminine warrior in our fight against fear.

In these chapters you will find words of courage and stories of broken beliefs and long-suppressed untold truths. You will find inspiration and guidance on how to rediscover and unleash your fierce wildness so you can live a fully embodied life—in your Truth—as a Divine warrior, honoring both your masculine and feminine energy. In these pages you will find yourself awakening, expanding, rising.

This book is for every woman who has felt a yearning of doubt deep within her heart that maybe she isn't living up to her true purpose . . . perhaps she is meant for something more than "just" being a wife, a mother, and a friend. Perhaps it's the realization that success and happiness don't live on a linear path, nor does that path look or feel the same for everyone. And being put together, staying organized, and plastering a smile on her face is overrated and exhausting. This is not the life she desires. This certainly isn't the life she envisioned for herself. And somewhere in the process of playing into the old paradigm, she lost touch with herself. Her soul. Her wild. Her heart.

She yearns for more, and she even glimpses it in those few moments when she allows herself to come undone. The beauty in her sobbing. The grace in her breakdown. The power in her unraveling. In these moments she witnesses the Goddess within, this woman who is magnetic, who can silence a room in a second, who knows exactly what she wants and is willing to live in alignment with that vision.

In that yearning is a craving; a craving for something deeper, wilder, more primal. A craving to live as a Goddess, a healer, a feminine warrior of light, love, and all that is pure.

Can you feel it in your bones?
Can you see yourself in her?

Are you nodding your head and tightly clutching the book or your e-reader as you read these words? Good!

Because this lifetime of doubt, this consistent inkling of disappointment within yourself, is an awakening. These words are activating a deep-seated desire that has always been yours but never had the space to truly be heard or felt. These words are drawing out what has been suffocated for years. You are living at your Awakening Crossroads: a cloudy, vague time in life right before a soul-expanding inner shift. Feel that excitement bubbling up within you at the prospect of change. Notice your heart pound faster as you consider what lives in the depths of your heart and soul. What if all those deep-rooted, silent desires you've felt over the years were able to manifest and become you, your reality, your life?

These pages hold visceral truths, concepts, and tools you will need to move from your Awakening Crossroads into true inner empowerment. You will learn why you feel this yearning deep within you. You will realize that every desire you have, even things you never thought were possible, were silenced and unable to surface because of the primal fear of societal outcasting and social segregation.

Through the lens of intimate stories of breakdown and triumph, the messiness of being human, and the thoughts and fears from my most insecure moments, you will learn exactly what I leaned on with every fiber of my being to uncover my Truth, re-wild my inner warrior, and live proud of the woman I am choosing to be every single day. Use this book, these words, as an invitation to begin awakening to your Truth, to write your own story, and to anoint yourself as the true Goddess you already are.

Our journey together begins with a hard truth: Everything that has gotten you to where you are now will NOT get you to where you desire to be.

Let me say that again. **Everything that has gotten you to where you are now will NOT get you to where you desire to be.**

Because where you are going is NOT where you have been. Humanity, our collective consciousness, has NOT been here before. It's a whole new world. A brand new experience. We are craving softness and quiet, calm, sweet moments of love and connection, unexplained joy, and pockets of happiness bursting throughout the day. We desire an abundance of time, fun, and freedom from our schedules and space to simply breathe, be present, and feel alive. We desire to live a life of love, not a life of striving, earning, proving, and pushing. We desire to live a life that flows seamlessly in aligned synchronicity; we want an effortless way of being.

This life isn't birthed from forcing and pushing your previous agenda and making sure everything happens in accordance with your meticulously mapped out plan. No, Goddess, this life manifests from surrender, from letting go, from trusting yourself and the Universe, and from finding your way back to love.

And that's why you're here: to learn how to fall back in love with yourself and your life and to identify as the true feminine warrior you are in your heart—fighting fire with love, anger with compassion, frustration with peace, and destruction with a higher vision of consciousness and joy.

Learn simple alignment techniques and perspective shifts so you can tap into your intuitive wisdom and learn to lead, grow, and evolve as a whole being. By following your inner guidance and using the tools provided in the final section of this book, learn how to balance your masculine and feminine energy centers and create a life of deep harmony and bliss. Open your consciousness and start allowing yourself to cultivate a wildly empowering perspective. Give yourself permission on every level to experience seemingly effortless opportunities and prosperity, to have immense joy and freedom, and to grow into your true purpose: to be a leader of love, kindness, and a beacon of radiant light for humanity.

Women across the globe are still subscribing to the same belief pattern that we must live a certain way and be a certain type of person to be successful, to be accepted by society, and to be happy. It's this box—this conforming to a belief system that is ancient and obsolete— that causes our own inner turmoil and perpetuates the explosive breakdown of society as we know it.

As women, we have forgotten how innately powerful we are.

We are wholeheartedly committed to reproducing the exact same experience we see other women struggling with. We believe that for *us,* it will be different. Somehow, we have convinced ourselves that we have the magical fairy dust required to have an insanely successful career, raise perfectly poised and highly intelligent children with impeccable manners, cook wholesome meals for our family on the daily, and be a wild, exotic woman who loves all things luxurious, sexy, and erotic in the bedroom (oh, and did I forget, we must always have smooth shaved legs, colored hair, and perfect eyebrows), PLUS make time to meditate, practice yoga, journal, send out holiday cards, and be a kind and loving human at all times. Yah, sure . . . you've got the magical fairy dust to make that happen. How exhausting, truly!

OR

Perhaps your expectations (that have been influenced by decades of societal conditioning and toxic patterning and disillusionment) are a tad out of alignment with the reality of what your body and mind actually desire, yah?

But that's easier to write about than to actually do the *do,* if you know what I mean. That twinge of worry when someone pops by unannounced and your house is a disaster, that subtle nod of disapproval from your coworker when your Casual Friday outfit is a little too casual, that fear that if you turn down one more girls' night out you'll officially be uninvited from the group . . . these are REAL social fears that we often face. Even if they seem ridiculous and irrational now that you read them, you can relate, can't you? Of course you can, because you are human, just like I am, and none of us were born immune to the influence of society.

So the question is this: How do we subscribe to a new belief pattern when our mind is riddled with fear?

That's what this book and my life's work as an intuitive life coach is all about: uncovering the fears that live beneath the surface and hide themselves in the "it's just a glass of wine and Netflix kind of night."

To live an extraordinary life and empower yourself to act toward your desired reality, you first need to understand what stands between who you are currently and who you desire to be: empowered, aligned, and free!

In the first three sections we will dive deep into the world of self-sabotage, silent traumas, and exploring your Goddess energy. You will explore your fears, how they have come to be, and the subtle ways in which they rule your life and work. You will then determine if you are, in fact, ready to shift beyond them. Here we explore the ideas of patriarchy, external validation, negative body image, the role of intimate relationships, and feminine superpowers like intuition, emotional resiliency, and energy healing.

In the fourth section we expand on how you can intentionally apply this knowledge and newfound clarity into your day to day. You will begin to see yourself as a leader of this collective shift into balancing the masculine and feminine, awakening your personal healing potential, and understanding your soulful responsibility. We will have fun looking into concepts like the common denominator of your life, how softness creates strength, what it means to be in energetic alignment with your desires, and a powerful tool: manifestation.

The final section of this book is about ACTION. A key part of truly living an embodied and aligned life is mastering tools and techniques that work for you. While we may share many similarities, our physical and energetic makeup can be quite unique, which is why it's important to honor our own experience with these tools and listen to our body. The wisdom is in the whispers. This section is designed to be your soulful tool kit. Have this book nearby and turn to it whenever you find yourself pulled into the darkness of doubt, worry, and fear. Know that with this knowledge and these tools, you have access to all that you need to step through your Awakening Crossroads and into your Feminine Warrior!

My desire for you is to feel excited, empowered, and enlightened on reclaiming your strength, your life, your Truth. Don't look at these tools and tips as yet another thing to add to your morning routine. It's not the actual doing that matters; rather, it's who you are being while you're doing the things that matter most. Simply put, *being* makes the *doing* much more powerful. Can you see that difference? The external output doesn't actually matter; it's the internal motivation and intention that is the driving force of the change.

While it may seem simple, this shift IS THE WORK! It is subtle and POWERFUL! And with this book in your hands (or ears), you have access to everything required to create this shift. I have complete faith that from these emotional frameworks, mindset techniques, and daily tools you will not only BE empowered, but you will also FEEL empowered . . . and really, that's what it's all about.

> *"The world will be saved by the Western Woman."*
> ~Dalai Lama

"It is time to reclaim our
connection
with Shakti (power),
innate wisdom (intuition),
and ferocious, unconditional love."

~Rebecca Campbell, Rise Sister Rise:
A Guide to Unleashing the Wise, Wild Woman Within

Section One

SUBTLE SELF-SABOTAGE

February 13, 2019

Dear Self,

Please stop striving so hard. You are doing an amazing job of being you, exactly as you are. It's important that you grant yourself time and space to truly learn all the things. You are a spiritual teacher. You are here to share your wisdom. It comes from playing, from trying, from failing, from crying, from living—truly living—every day.
Focus less on your output and more on your input. How can you serve more externally by spending time internally? Accept where you are and LOVE who you are. In this moment. In all moments.

This is it.
This is the journey.
Your journey.
Live it.
Love it.
Simply Be.

xo
Dea

I have always been a good girl . . . the kind of girl who got straight As in school, not because I loved learning, but because I loved the praise and support that came along with them. I was a master at following the rules. As a teenager, my curfew was midnight. I was home every night at midnight. On the dot. I thrived in this world of strict black and white because I knew how to get what I needed: love, affection, attention, and at the root of it all, validation.

I knew I wanted to be successful. And I knew that in order to be so, I would need to earn a great income, at a great job, doing something relatively interesting. I would need to buy a great house, marry a great guy, birth great kids, and live a great life. My definition of success? Work hard. Earn money. Follow the rules. Check all the boxes. And be happy.

And, in essence, I did it. I did most of the things I set out to do. The problem was that I wasn't happy. I was constantly sick. I was exhausted. I was uninterested in my own life. I was fantasizing about faraway lands where I'd live by the beach and tend to a garden and spend afternoons relaxing with friends over iced tea and evenings dancing in the moonlight in my bare feet. I'd have space in my day to have afternoon sex, leisurely prepare a healthy, nourishing meal, and sit and discuss topics like love, space, evolution, consciousness, connection, and freedom. I had a vision in my mind that created happiness, and my life was the furthest thing from it.

The realization that my ideal life and actual reality were so far from each other was when I first became aware of how backward Western society is. I was doing all the things I was "meant" to do with the promise of joy and happiness at the end, but the end was nowhere in sight. It felt like I was in an endless cycle of Groundhog Day. Joy and happiness were nonexistent. I began to realize that maybe the plan I had been following since elementary school—CAPP class (Career and Personal Planning)—was actually leading me farther away from what I truly wanted. And what I wanted, so desperately, so deeply . . . what I chased all along was F R E E D O M.

By the sheer fact that you picked up this book I know that you, too, can relate to this desire and longing for something that feels outside your current reality. That dream of the sun on your face and full-belly laughter in the middle of the afternoon for no reason other than because it feels good. That vision of looking at your body—naked, exposed, and free—and feeling complete reverence for the magic that is your natural being. That desire to know, believe, and *feel* what your purpose is, why you're alive, and what you're meant to experience and share during this lifetime. *This* is what you're craving; *this* is what lights up that part of your soul you've ignored for so long and are tired of pretending doesn't exist. *This* is what gives you a tingling sensation throughout your whole body at even the mere thought that a life complete with all your desires *might* be possible for *you.*

My love, I am here to share with you that it is. It IS possible for you. And if you are ready, together we are going to explore how.

First, let's take a look at who you identify as today.

Perhaps you are quite good at achieving goals. Heck, you might as well change your name to goal-getting, trend-setting, and high-achieving woman, right? You set your mind to something and pride yourself on being able to achieve it, often in record timing.

You have a superb track record of always excelling in your career. You spend countless hours at your computer desk, slogging away while you ward off those feelings of overwhelm and exhaustion because "work hard, play hard." Right? After all, the end result is what matters most.

Or maybe you've dedicated your life to your children, pining over Pinterest boards at night while the kids are asleep, desiring to be *that* mom who comes up with fun and inventive new crafts and projects, the Instagram-worthy meal preps, and more. But exhaustion and burnout threatens to spill over, and the only way you quell those feelings each night is with a glass of Pinot Grigio in one hand while you Netflix and chill. In solitude, of course. After all, the last thing you want to do is to cuddle an adult baby after having children hanging off you all day.

Regardless of which end of the spectrum of external achievement you're on, let's get one thing straight: You are an expert at *doing all the things*!

You somehow manage to maintain a decent balance in the household while juggling your work life and daily to-do list, fitting in a workout, keeping the toilet paper stocked, and putting out fires around every corner. You eventually collapse onto your couch at the end of the day with little to no affection or attention left for your partner or yourself.

And that's just on Tuesday!

Friend, I bow down to you.

You are the epitome of a modern woman living her life to the fullest!

At least the "socially acceptable" version of a full life. But that's where the problem is.

Everything you're doing is for everyone else.

But what about you?

Have you ever noticed that?

All the late nights at the office, the replying to emails after hours, the working through your lunch hour . . . it's all for someone else, isn't it?

And how about those billions of loads of laundry you've done in your day? Is that really for you or for everyone else who benefits from the restocked dressers you're providing?

Look, I'm not saying to stop doing these things, I'm just asking if you have ever noticed that you are really good at doing all the things for all the people?

I have a question for you: Are you happy? Like truly, madly, deeply happy? Because I have a feeling you might not be. I have a feeling you are at a point in your life where everything on the outside looks "right," looks successful, looks put together, but when you are honest with yourself, you feel lost, sad, broken, unsure, and like something is missing.

You are so talented at doing all the things to keep everyone else happy, but when you spend time with yourself, in quiet reflection (albeit for even ten minutes while you're hiding out in the bathroom trying to catch a break from your kids), and you ask yourself, "What makes me happy?," the answer to that question likely eludes you.

FIRST OF ALL, YOU ARE NOT ALONE.
Please do not let that annoying tricky Ego step in here and flood you with guilt, worry, self-doubt, and a sense of overwhelm. You are not doing anything wrong. You are not a bad mom, or a bad wife, or a bad manager, or a bad community member, or a bad recycler, or a bad anything.

> You are simply a woman existing in a reality that values and prioritizes productivity and outcomes over joy and happiness.

So throughout our time together, whenever you feel that Ego rise, please do me a favor and say this out loud: "Hey, Ego! You're not invited to this party; please see yourself out now."

SECONDLY, I WANT YOU TO KNOW THAT LIFE DOESN'T HAVE TO BE THIS WAY.
It is possible for you to create massive perspective shifts in the way you think, speak, react, and act that translate to amazing amounts of joy, happiness, freedom, and love every day. And it doesn't have to be a lot of work. I get it; you're already operating at a 10/10 for capacity.

I've been helping women tap into this internal strength for years, and now I want to do the same for you! Buckle up, sunshine, we're about to have quite the ride.

THE CURSE OF THE
MODERN WOMAN

For just a moment, stop and take a long, deep pause.

Close your eyes and breathe in, all the way to the bottom of your lungs. Feel the expansion of your ribcage as your abdomen fills with fresh oxygen, fresh prana, fresh energy.

Stay with your breath for a few moments as you calm your nervous system and settle into this present moment.

This entire chapter addresses some deep core fears and wounds that we as a collective society hold within our subconscious. It's okay if you feel overwhelmed or agitated, frustrated or annoyed. You are awakening from within, which is why this book is alive and breathing . . . to awaken the parts of you that are not yet aware; to awaken the ability you possess within your own mind and body to heal, to love, to feel joy.

Remember how you're really good at doing all the things for other people? Well, if you're like most modern women, that means you have dedicated your entire existence to someone else. You have placed all your metrics of joy, happiness, and satisfaction of self in the hands of another being. You have created a pattern of constantly needing approval and validation for the work you've chosen to do or the children you devote every second of your every day to in order to feel like a human of value.

And when you don't get what you need from others, you do one of two things:

1. You shut down, become reclusive, go inward, and use wine, TV, TikTok, anything to help you drift off to a world where you feel loved, valued, and seen.

2. You pick a fight over nothing. You bring up old issues even when they aren't bothering you; you nag, you nitpick, you do anything you can do to get some form of attention from others.

It sounds harsh, right? I know, it is! And believe me when I say you are NOT ALONE in this.

It is incredibly common, and sadly, not talked about. Until now.

As women, we are natural caregivers and have a deep desire to nourish and give in every way possible. We learned this behavior from our mothers, our aunts, and our older sisters, and internalized it by watching the choices of every single woman we were surrounded by as children and teenage girls. We saw them give everything they had, always putting everyone else first. We watched them work long hours at their job, come home and feed the family, clean the house on weekends, buy gifts for birthdays, help with school projects, and maybe, once in a while, get a moment to paint their own toenails. We love and value our elders, we look to them for guidance, and we emulate what we see. Thus, this constant giving and doing and putting others first became our measure of *how to be a good woman*.

ENTER THE CURSE OF THE MODERN WOMAN

- We get ourselves into trouble in our inability to give to ourselves.

- We *need* that raise or promotion to feel validated.

- We *need* the approval of the other moms at morning drop-off to feel like we are in the "in crowd."

- We *need* our children to behave like perfect little angels at Claire's birthday party so we'll avoid being judged as a "bad mom."

- We *need* to lose those extra ten pounds to be seen and valued as a woman.

- We *need* the consistency of nagging our partner to "pick up your socks" every freaking week because it fuels our belief that the world will collapse (or at least be dirty) without us. This belief makes us feel important and valued.

Each of these situations has been created to fulfill our internal need of validation and love. But what happens when we don't get that raise? Or when we eat the whole cake? Or when we end up screaming at our partner over nothing? Or when we scream at our kids?

Then what?
Then what do others believe about us?
Then what do *we* believe about *ourselves*?

In my years of getting down and dirty with women's subconscious beliefs and fears, a big one that comes up regularly is the "L" word: the utter fear of being judged as L A Z Y.

Yep, I said it. We, as a collective, are terrified that others (especially other women) will deem us lazy and therefore, a useless piece of garbage and wasted space.

I'll give you **one** guess as to why we have this subconscious belief so deeply ingrained in our psyche.

Mmm hmm, decades and decades of the patriarchy ruling our lives.

Before you decide that this is a man-hating, power-bashing book of feminism, let me stop you. When I say the patriarchy, what I mean is the imbalanced rise of masculine energy.

I do not mean men.
I do not mean corporate businesses.
I mean masculine energy.

As a quick crash course on energy, you need to know that every living being has both masculine and feminine energy. It is not restricted to just one gender—all men have both, all women have both, all non-gender-identified humans have both. This is not an us-against-them situation. It's an ALL-of-us situation.

Through colonization, the industrial revolution, and the feminist movement, we created an environment of high masculine energy. We, as Western society, began idolizing the attributes of masculine energetic traits—things like productivity, problem solving, physical strength, linear time, and a "can-do" attitude—while using control and power and self-induced guilt to produce more results. These are the attributes that our culture gravitated toward. And clung to! *And sadly, many of us still cling to heavy masculine energetics even today. It's how we define ourselves. The energetic harmony of the Earth is severely imbalanced because the feminine is severely imbalanced.* And rightfully so.

Over the last few centuries and decades, we have cultivated our lives as we know them: massive advances in technology, science, medicine, etc. We truly would not be where we are today without this shift. Nor would you be able to read this book on your Kindle or listen on Audible or secretly stalk your children on TikTok.

However, what we have also created in the process is a loss of feminine energy, and even more so, an utter disregard for it or even villainizing it to the point of desperate suppression.

We started viewing feminine energetic traits
as weak, airy, whimsical, soft, witchy, magical,
and with a lack of boundaries or direction.
We started validating <u>only</u> the masculine
and chastising the feminine—demonizing,
shaming, and suffocating it.

Hence, the incessant need to be seen as anything but lazy. If you are lazy, you are not producing, creating, pushing, forcing, doing; you are stagnant and boring. A total waste of space. Thus, our collective view for quite some time.

You know those hippie friends you have from college? The ones who have traveled around the world for years, wearing flowy, earthy clothes, living by the beach in their camper van and generally not taking any responsibility for their own futures? You know the feelings of judgment you have toward them? They're the same as your subconscious judgments toward your own feminine energy. Feminine energy is unnecessary, lazy, slow, too sensitive, too wishy-washy, and doesn't get you ahead in life. Sound familiar?

So, circling back to the idea that you have dedicated your entire existence to someone else, the reason you don't feel satisfied, content, or happy is a lack of connection and belief in your feminine energy.

That's the ENTIRE REASON for this book.

To bring you back into alignment with who you truly are.

To recalibrate into both energetic levels at all times: a woman of both masculine AND feminine energy; a woman who can both "get it all done" and "surrender to receive intuitive guidance."

You are already *both*. The latter is just buried under a few layers of social patriarchal conditioning that we're going to peel back together.

The question I want you to ponder is *How do we subscribe to new belief patterns when these older fears are currently ruling our minds?*

The answer lies in the future pages of this book.

Stick with me, Goddess, and we'll find our way together.

"I have never,
EVER met anyone
who's regretted following
their heart."

~Marie Forleo,
Everything Is Figureoutable

EXHAUSTION AND GUILT

The Divine Feminine has a natural ability to intuitively solve problems with ease, to effortlessly manage multiple things at once, and to be completely present with the intimate joys of life.

She is the foundation of culture, of stories, of connection, of community.

She is most content in a state of flow without heavily constricted rules and guidelines, free to dance and play through life while expressing her love, creativity, and wisdom whenever the desire arises.

In this natural state the Feminine is most powerful.

She is seductive, influential, and inviting.

She always receives what she wants, simply by being present.

It is not what she says or what she does that produces results, it is her energetic presence being felt, witnessed, and known.

She loves to be seen.

She loves to be wanted, lusted after, and desired.

She is magnetic, energetically calling to her all her desires as she dances with the wind and bows down to smell the fragrant flowers of life.

YOU ARE THE FEMININE AND THE FEMININE IS YOU.
Have you ever paused to consider that we women are natural birthers, creators, nurturers? And yet we continue to self-sabotage our successes and desires as women because we are too busy subscribing to a wounded masculine energetic paradigm. We suppress our creativity, our fluidity, our desires, and our dreams. We dim our voices, hide our truths, and, on many occasions, we run ourselves into the ground playing puppet to everyone else. Women have the ability to create and birth life—literally and figuratively. That is creativity defined with a capital C. And as you know, the environment has to be just right, it has to find that sweet spot, to allow creation to occur.

So when you slog it at the computer for twelve hours a day, when you work yourself into oblivion to produce results and prove that your value is undeniable, when you deny yourself joy because you're too exhausted from your day of pleasing everyone else . . . I mean, it gets a little complicated to be creative and in feminine flow, no?

Add in the incessant guilt that runs through your mind when you don't get everything on your to-do list done. The constant worry that you aren't doing enough, for yourself, for your family, for the environment, and the agony you feel over what you'll look like in your bathing suit this summer, all of it is an output of energy dedicated to a paradigm that no longer serves any part of you. And yet you stay true to it because it's familiar. It's comfortable. It's what you've always known.

CREATIVITY IS YOUR LIFE EXPRESSION—A WAY OF LIVING, BREATHING, AND BEING.

Creativity is one of our most magical gifts as we embody our feminine energy. As women, we are designed to prep and prepare the right environment for our creativity to flow. This creativity is about birthing and nurturing children, developing ideas and concepts, learning hands-on skills, building energy in our bodies to feel vibrant and alive, being inspired to plan a trip to Europe, and completing tasks with ease, all in a joyful, fulfilled, and peaceful manner. It's about living life in a state of flow. It's about allowing new ideas and solutions to find their way to you instead of seeking the "next best thing." It's a powerful way to live as it requires less input and naturally produces an output with more impact. This is your feminine creativity, and it comes naturally for you, even if it doesn't feel like it.

Embodying your feminine energy is about releasing and receiving to create the ideal environment. It requires releasing attachment to anything that feels restrictive, allowing your needs to be met through effortless receiving (from others, yourself, and the Divine). It's living in a state of fluid creativity. This ideal environment looks different for every woman, and it's essential that you get curious and explore what yours is.

For you, this environment may look and feel like spending evenings on the couch in solitude, being quiet, calm, and decompressing after your day. Or perhaps it means having time away from work to be social, playing, laughing, and enjoying others. Or maybe it means having a powerful support network like a coach or mentor who holds you through it all.

Take a few moments and reflect on your ideal environment:

🖊 When do you feel most fluid and free, uninhibited, and open to creativity?

_____

_____

_____

🖊 What time of day do you receive your creative downloads or thoughts?

_____

_____

_____

🖊 What does creativity mean to you, and how do you love to express yourself?

_____

_____

_____

Write down your answers so that when you forget and get too busy again, you can reflect and remember that you are most powerful and full of impact when you are adhering to your natural feminine flow.

Without this ideal environment, there is no space for your creativity to flow. It's like a kinked garden hose—you are doing your best to ensure your front lawn and garden is watered. Then you decide you want to do your neighbor a favor and water their grass and garden. You have beautiful, generous thoughts with which to start your day, except you have a problem. Your garden hose has a kink in it, and it's stopping the flow of water. Until you address the kink and untwist it, which can take some time and patience, water won't flow freely and abundantly. You need to address the root of the problem, not just treat it at a surface level. Now try to apply this analogy to your life. What subconscious self-sabotage patterns do you allow yourself to partake in day after day that lead to you and your body feeling heavy, lethargic, empty, unfulfilled, and downright terrible?

If you want to have more creativity and feminine flow in your life, you must learn to connect more deeply with your feminine wisdom and intuition. It truly is the shift that will get your juices flowing, both physically and figuratively. And lucky for us, every story, message, and resource in this book is designed to support you to step more deeply into your feminine flow.

Make a commitment to yourself now:

I, _____, choose to release the

heaviness of exhaustion, of guilt, of worry, fear, and

doubt. I know that I am already doing enough. I know

that I am deeply loved, I am deeply supported, and

I am deeply valued. I will no longer subscribe to the

belief that my daily to-do list rules my life. Instead, I

choose moments of joy, moments of connection, and a

lifetime of love.

_____

EXTERNAL VALIDATION

Since the beginning of time, humans have been designed to belong to a tribe, a collective, a group of people. Any deviation from clan, tribe, or collective rules automatically results in ostracization and shaming. Add in the primal need for acceptance, acknowledgment, and validation, and pair that with centuries' worth of patriarchal conditioning, and what do we have? A recipe for perfect disaster for both women and men. Our worth is now measured by the amount of pressure we can live with, perform under, and deliver results within.

Throughout the years (and centuries) of suppressing our feminine energy and training ourselves to embody our masculine *doer* mentality, we have learned to dampen our natural intuitive gifts. We have taught ourselves as a society to be excellent at doing all the things:

✓ Managing the household.
✓ Earning as much as our partner.

- ✓ Working 8+ hours a day and still making a wholesome-*ish* meal every night.
- ✓ Taking everyone to their weekend sports and activities on our days off.
- ✓ Keeping the guest bed clean and made just in case someone pops by unannounced.
- ✓ Shopping organic. Then feeling too broke. So shopping non-organic, but local! Then finding that's too much work. Thus, going to Walmart and feeling guilty about it the whole time, wondering how anyone else manages their internal guilt while staying on a budget.

With your mind and emotions constantly feeling like they are forever locked in a never-ending minefield, can you see why you've lost connection with your Self? Can you see why you may have gained a few extra pounds recently? Can you see why you turn to Netflix to numb you to sleep at night? Can you see why the thought of being intimate with your partner is often the farthest thing from your mind?

We are so focused on *doing all the things* that we have no space or time to simply BE. And *being* is the essence of the Feminine. The Divine Feminine is about being in the present moment, experiencing the delight of being alive, resting in quiet contemplation as Universal wisdom flows in, rejoicing in nature, and witnessing the magic of life.

Ultimately, the Divine Feminine is your worst nightmare when you're strung out in overwhelm and all you can see is that looming list of responsibilities and requirements that fall on your shoulders, knowing full well that if you ask anyone else to help you it will become a bigger mess than it already is, and you'll be the one cleaning up that mess.

I get it. It can be very challenging to embody the Feminine when we are so focused on what needs to get done. We are conditioned to believe that it is more important to earn as much or more than our male partner than to contemplate our reason for existence and our purpose for being alive. The belief that our worth as a woman lies in whether the laundry is clean and the fridge is stocked, rather than our innate ability to command the room with our magnetic grace. The belief that our natural intuitive gifts are simply a coincidence, even though we KNEW that situation was going to occur and could have saved everyone a lot of heartache and pain.

Women are conditioned to suppress their feminine. It's been indoctrinated into your whole body that you need to be more like him—him being masculine energy—in order to be worthy and validated in this world.

Excuse my language, but F*** THAT!

We are allowing this social conditioning to produce hate, frustration, and aggravation toward our very being. By denying our natural feminine gifts, we are truly missing out on the most blissful experiences of life, which is the primary reason we are constantly in a state of unease and discontentment even though on paper, our life isn't so bad.

If we seek validation from people and things outside of us, including the sweet satisfaction of accomplishing our to-do list at the expense of our health and mental sanity, we are focusing our precious energetic output on our external environment, thus producing those familiar feelings of misery, fear, lack, and guilt. Alternatively, when we turn our attention inward, when we become curious about our innate wisdom and intuitive gifts, when we take moments to pause and be fully present with our experience of life, we welcome in feelings of peace, calm, contentment, joy, and fulfillment.

This concept is the same with our incessant desire to consume materialistic things. We believe that each new purchase will bring us closer to the contentment and joy that we seek from within. That a mani-pedi, a new dress, and new patio furniture will be the answer to our prayers. But when we fill the internal void with external things, we simply expand the void . . . *and usually go further into debt at the same time.* Buying more things, having a bigger house, and subscribing to every TV-streaming platform won't equate a higher level of happiness. It often results in more guilt, more relationship issues, and more looming debt. It's not the purchases themselves that are the problem, however; it's the belief that you *need them to be happy and fulfilled* that causes the disconnect.

You know that concept of *keeping up with the Joneses*—the idea that your household should have all that your neighbors and friends have, and more, in order to maintain your social status?

It's the caving to your children's wishes for every new gaming console to mask your pain that your preteen is starting to pull away from you. It's the sneaky judgment in your head that says you can't wear the same dress to two different weddings unless it's a completely different group of friends or you'll suffer the silent wrath of judging eyes. It's the conversations with friends that help you to see how much better your life will be with a brand new car, even though yours is paid off and running fine. Unless you are willing to shift your perspective and anchor your intention behind the purchases, you will continue to feel the same way you did before, with or without the things.

When you change the way you think and feel inside, your external world begins to reflect these changes.

You've heard it before and I'm going to say it again . . .

Everything you desire already exists within you.

Sounds crazy, right? I know, I thought so too. This concept used to really bother me because I couldn't wrap my head around it. I'd think to myself: *If everything I desire and need is already within me, why don't I have it . . . right now?!* I spent hours reading spiritual self-help books, learning the principles and concepts behind manifestation and living a purposeful life, and yet my life looked nothing like I could see in my head. I was tired, annoyed, quick to judge, and constantly feeling broke.

So what does this concept truly mean?

Everything you desire already exists within you.

Let's break it down.

Everything you desire—this relates to the aspects of you at a deeper level than simply things you want. These are your core fundamental desires like love, health, connection, and purpose. Do you desire to make a big difference in this world? Do you desire to live a simple and beautiful life? Do you desire to feel strong and agile until your late nineties?

Already exists—when you look into quantum physics, you learn that there are different times, spaces, and dimensions in our Universe. We, humanity, are currently living in the third dimension and are slowly making an accession toward the fourth and fifth dimensions. What this means is that in other times, spaces, and dimensions there is a version of you who already is making a big difference in the world, who is living a simple and beautiful life, who already is strong and agile. She already exists, she's just not manifested in this third dimension. Don't worry, we'll go into this idea more deeply later on.

Within you—your internal reaction to every moment in life is what creates your reality. It's not the physical situations that you have that determine what your life is like, *it's how you feel about them.* Your thoughts and feelings about everything dictate your life. Each of us experience situations differently, as everything is filtered through our minds. For example, you and your sister may have completely different memories of family Christmas in 1990. Maybe you remember fun, laughter, and lots of presents, while your sister, who's a few years older, remembers the late-night fight your parents had and has never been able to forget it. You both were at the same Christmas celebration, but your reality of it was different.

Two individuals can have the SAME external situation, but it is their internal reaction to the situation that creates their reality of calm or chaos. Every single one of us has this ability and power in our lives. Thus, investing in yourself is the best investment with the highest return on investment you'll ever receive.

When you change the way you think inside, you change how your world looks out there.

The reality of above statement is based on the Law of Attraction, but we'll dive into that one a bit later. For now, just know that this IS possible for you, and by the end of this book, you'll understand why and how!

To start shifting the way you think internally, you need to first understand two nasty culprits that keep us stuck in our less-than-desirable environments: judgment and avoidance.

"The root cause of all judgment is the fear of not being good enough, not being worthy of love, and not being safe."

~Gabrielle Bernstein, Judgment Detox:
Release the Beliefs That Hold You
Back from Living a Better Life

JUDGMENT

One of the main reasons our external environment doesn't reflect peace, calm, and joy every day is due to our internal dialogue. Judgment is a nasty habit that genuinely strips away your connection to your feminine flow and eats away at your self-confidence and self-belief. It's a sneaky aspect of our Ego that can be so convincing that it takes over our entire inner dialogue.

Judgment flows in two ways:

1. Judgment toward others: For instance, perhaps you have a few friends who have partnered with some direct sales companies, and every time you see a post from them on social media you think to yourself, "They are so rude for posting about their new products so much on Facebook."

2. Judgment toward yourself: "Why am I not as fit or thin as they are? Why am I not farther along in my business? Why am I always so awkward in social settings?"

Judgment is one of the biggest thieves of our joy and happiness. It robs us of being in the present moment, and when we allow it to really gain momentum, we can easily step into *comparisonitis*: a nasty form of self-judgment against others.

Have you read Gabrielle Bernstein's book from 2018 called *Judgment Detox*? I bought it because I like Gabby's writing even though I didn't believe I was a judgmental person. But I knew there must be something valuable in the concept if she wrote an entire book on it. My intention was to explore Gabby's teachings to better support my clients when judgment came up in sessions. I respect Gabby as a writer and teacher, so I purchased the book despite these thoughts: *I am a positive, sunny-outlook person, and I am NOT in need of a book teaching me how to stop judging others, but surely this can help someone else.*

The book arrived in my mailbox mid-winter, and I can remember one morning sitting cozily on my couch, sipping a cup of tea as I opened it. I felt my surprisingly common cynicism and preconceived notions about how this book wasn't for me. I felt self-righteous in the fact that I was merely reading it as "research" for future clients who would need my support to move out of judgment.

As it turns out, I was a judgment machine—I doled out judgments as though I was Oprah back in the day: "YOU get a judgment and

YOU get a judgment and YOU get a judgment!"

I did the work Gabby asked us to do in the book: I wrote out all the people and all the things I was judging. You know who I was judging most?

My friends!

I was judging some of my best friends at our local yoga studio because I felt they were *more successful yoga teachers* than I was. I felt so insecure in my own success and impact as a yoga teacher that I judged some of my favorite human beings! I mean, come on! These were some of my closest and dearest friends—the friends I invited to my wedding and shared intimate secrets with. Why on earth would I allow myself to judge them and their success so viciously?

Why? Because I was scared. I felt inadequate next to them. I felt unworthy when I measured my external success with theirs. I was jealous and sad because I didn't believe in myself as much as they appeared to believe in themselves. I was convinced that they were better human beings than I was because their classes were full and mine were not.

It was in this process that I learned how powerful our judgments can be and how they guide our way to internal growth and expansion. I was sad and frustrated that I wasn't a more influential and sought-after yoga teacher in my community, so I judged those who were. And here's the kicker: I was a *brand new* yoga teacher, fresh off my 200-hour training. Of course I wasn't a more sought-after teacher . . . I was new! I was still honing my skills. I was finding my groove. But instead of offering myself compassion and love during this journey, I pushed my discomfort onto others and blamed them for taking all the success away from me—this act is our societal *lack mentality* in full effect.

Lack mentality is the idea that if one has success or money or joy, there is now less for everyone else. Note: It is completely FALSE! It's a concept that has been developed and enforced by Ego-centered leaders throughout the centuries to promote fear in humanity in order to keep us from believing in ourselves. If we believe that there is only room for a select few to experience the success, money, and joy we desire, we are easily influenced. It becomes much easier to believe the fabricated lies told by others about how to get there, what to buy to speed up the process, and all the ways we are doing it wrong. It keeps us in line like sheep, always looking outside ourselves for guidance and validation, which we now know is a culprit of our discontentment.

My journey of releasing judgment began to look like this: I spent time journaling and pondering, asking myself a ridiculous amount of questions such as:

- What would it be like to simply *witness* their success as a desire within myself to experience the same?
- What would it feel like to realize that they are mirroring my potential and my desire?
- How can I train myself to focus on embodying these qualities within myself instead of feeling a sense of lack because of my perceived inability to create what they have?

When I started to focus on the oneness between us, the oneness of their dreams and mine, it became easier to release my attachment to judgment and destructive self-talk. It allowed me to see their success as my potential and their output as a reflection of my journey. It created so much more peace within me that I could stop harboring the secret guilt within myself that I had a terrible addiction to judging my friends. Thank you, Ms. Gabby B for that life changer! And thank you to my own triggers and judgments for pointing me in my perfect direction to heal.

Where are you allowing judgments of others to steal your joy?

How can you start using those judgments as a roadmap for your desired experience?

Judgment is not always present in an outward fashion. In fact, a large percentage of our judgmental thoughts are directed toward ourselves. That inner mean girl thrives on negative self-talk. We are our own worst critics, and we are nasty to ourselves. I don't think any of us would keep a friend or partner around who talked to us or treated us the way we treat ourselves: criticizing our every move, every thought; undermining and undercutting ourselves; belittling ourselves and our journey.

I saw an ad years ago. Women were asked to write down all the thoughts they had about themselves and their bodies on a daily basis. They were then asked to say these things out loud to their best friend on camera. I don't remember a single woman making it through her list without sobbing in sadness. We have this backward idea that what occurs in our mind is private and secret; therefore, it can be as degrading, brutal, and downright evil as we like. But the truth is, as you'll continue learning throughout this book, our thoughts are not secret. Our thoughts create our reality, and everything we experience in life reflects our internal landscape. The more you judge yourself, the more you'll feel judgment from others and feel comfortable judging them as well. It's a whole judgment cycle that stems from our own feelings of unworthiness. To reconnect to your feminine flow, you must first detach from the judgments (both external and internal) that keep you stuck in this cycle—judgments of your body, your career, your relationship, your emotions, your dreams and desires. All the damn things!

When it comes to our emotions, one powerful way to ease the judgment is to remember that they are surfacing within you for a reason. There is a purpose behind your emotions. To experience a mass array of emotions is a gift we possess, even though it can often feel like a curse. The more time you sit in the discomfort of the emotion, the more you learn about your subconscious beliefs and patterns that dictate your reality. These are the beliefs and patterns that keep you stuck in this negative judgment cycle, so this type of work may not be exactly *enjoyable*, but it is **essential**. Therefore, having an energetic support system of coaches, mentors, and friends, learning to create super solid boundaries, and using emotional release techniques like the ones you'll learn in this book are keys to your expansion.

WARRIOR WISDOM:

If judgment is a big part of your life, please spend extra time working with these two healing resources in the final section of this book: Mirror Gazing and Writing a Letter to Your Inner Child. These tools, when used consistently, will support your release of those judgmental thoughts and beliefs.

AVOIDANCE

Self-sabotage often manifests as avoidance, and avoidance has many names and faces. We create different mechanisms throughout our life to allow us to feel safe and protected, especially when faced with uncomfortable situations like job loss, divorce, grieving a loved one, or even simply being bored of our own life and not knowing how to change it.

We each have a number of specific patterns that we revert to in order to avoid situations and numb out. What we are actually avoiding is our emotional discomfort and dis-ease, but often we pretend it's simply to escape the pressures of day-to-day life. Some common avoidance techniques may seem super fun and harmless like drinking wine with girlfriends, scrolling through Facebook, or online shopping. These activities are harmless until they become patterns we use on autopilot when in emotional pain.

When I lived in the city in 2012 (I now live in a super small town and love it), I had a very prominent avoidance technique of solo shopping at the mall. I didn't have much money, so I rarely went to actually buy anything. But the act of aimlessly wandering the mall, trying on clothes and envisioning where I would wear them and who I'd be with and what it would feel like to own everything helped me escape my emotional discomfort. I was in complete denial of my emotional pain, all I knew was it felt good to escape the judgments of others and the worries and anxieties in my mind. And my priority was feeling good!

Years later when I moved to the small town I live in now, I had to face this pattern head on. With only two clothing shops to choose from, mindless shopping became obsolete, and I was finally forced to spend time sitting quietly in nature with my emotions. It took some time, but I became much more emotionally resilient and no longer used mindless shopping as an avoidance technique . . . until COVID-19!

Suddenly during the lockdown of 2020, this old pattern resurfaced. I had never been much of an online shopper prior to this time, but I noticed how easy it was for me to mindlessly browse my favorite stores online while sitting on the couch watching TV. I filled my cart at each site, took a pause, then purchased nothing because it was also a time of financial uncertainty. Within just a few weeks I realized how many hours I had spent with this avoidance technique. It took a global pandemic, coming back to watching the news every day (I stopped this habit years ago as it's far too depressing for a highly sensitive empath like me), and a lot of fear-based uncertainty for this avoidance technique to find its way back to me.

Perhaps you can relate?

Pause. Breathe. Reflect.

What are some common go-to activities when you're feeling overwhelmed and want to avoid dealing with those feelings?	
What are the mindless things you love to do that distract away from your pain, worries, anxiety, fear, sadness, or discomfort?	

There is absolutely no shame in these avoidance techniques; we all have them! The key is to identify what they are so when you feel the urge to do that thing, you can explore what the deep underlying emotion is that you're avoiding. This work is so empowering. It allows you to take back your power to actively and consciously choose how you move through your emotions and any situation that upsets you.

The urge to use your avoidance technique will usually arise when you feel helpless or a lack of control. Perhaps someone you care about is in pain and you can't do anything about it, or perhaps someone at work is triggering you and you're ready to smack them across the face, or perhaps a new project you just started is not gaining the traction you assumed it would. Situations like these breed the subtle sensation that makes you want to simultaneously run away, pull out your hair, and sob uncontrollably. But, as we've been exploring, our society doesn't value this emotional breakdown; therefore, we find an avoidance technique instead. [Enter your go-to technique here.]

Let's use my shopping addiction as an example of what happens over time when we continue to avoid our emotions: What I didn't know back in 2012 was that I was beginning my first real spiritual awakening process. Having no prior experience or awareness of what was occurring within me, or any real guidance or mentors to help me understand my own self, I just assumed I was going through a dark phase. It didn't even cross my mind that I might need some more solitude or quiet space to reflect on my own emotions and needs. I just saw shopping as an outlet. I was in my twenties at that time of my life, and I spent the majority of my days hanging out with friends, planning themed parties, and going on camping trips together. I spent ALL my time with roommates, friends, and boyfriends . . . rarely did I have actual time to myself for my own thoughts and emotional processing.

As it turns out, the solitude at the mall foreshadowed the deep introspective work I would later partake in when I hit rock bottom while living in New Zealand in 2013. I had become such an expert at avoidance that when I was living in New Zealand, experiencing all the symptoms and signs of depression and anxiety, I refused to see them for what they truly were. I used social media, alcohol, excessive exercising, and wallowing in self-pity (my new avoidance techniques) to avoid the reality of what I was feeling: sad, alone, unwanted, unloved, and utterly broken.

It took months and months of physical and emotional agony of avoiding my true emotions and blaming everyone else around me for my pain before I could finally witness and accept my deep inner expansion. It required me leaving New Zealand, going back to Canada, and finally looking at my own inner dialogue before I could start feeling whole again. And the mindless scrolling during the 2020 lockdown was a precursor for one of the darkest times in my life, and equally one of the most expansive spiritual awakenings I've ever experienced.

Our triggers, challenges, and avoidance techniques are all guideposts pointing us inward to our own expansion. It's our soul gently illuminating the pathway for us to come home to ourselves. It's our awareness of our own avoidance that saves our bodies and hearts from unnecessary pain. It's an observer view of our daily choices and actions that empowers us enough to ask for help. It's trusting in the tools and resources that we possess to rewrite our story and welcome in a joyous and happy experience despite the challenge.

We are here to acknowledge who and where we are today and make the conscious choice to step forward. To be the light in our own life. To forge our own path to healing both internally and externally. To come home to ourselves and live in harmony with our masculine and feminine energies. To choose love over fear, possibility over doubt, and growth over stagnation. To love, embodied, as the Feminine Warrior.

"Trust that your wounds are exactly as the Universe planned. They were divinely placed in your life in the perfect order so that you could show up for them with love and remember the light within."

~Gabrielle Bernstein,
*The Universe Has Your Back:
Transform Fear to Faith*

Section Two

UNAPOLOGETIC CONVERSATIONS

One of the most defeating manifestations of self-sabotage comes in the form of struggling with body image. It is virtually impossible to be a woman in today's world and not feel the pressure to look a specific way. You've likely seen my Instagram stories of me in a bikini, one day sitting with the pain of my deeply programmed self-worth issues, and other days, dancing in that same bikini, feeling empowered and beautiful. It's a constant, ongoing daily journey to reprogram this cultural conditioning, and it's a journey that we are all on together.

This subtle way of sabotaging our lives is in the very fabric of our being. It shows up in our choice to wear a one-piece at the beach instead of a bikini to avoid showing our stretch marks. It is in how we decide what to wear to an interview conducted by all men: nothing too sexy, nothing to blah—it has to be just right. It shows up in whether we post that family photo with all those laugh lines on full display, and in the feeling that arises when you see your postpartum body in full light.

And if you have your own business, I know you've felt the effects of wanting to use your body/face/lifestyle in your online marketing but feel uncomfortable because of how you look. Or perhaps you know your business will grow if you get behind that camera for a Facebook Live, but even just the thought brings you into a cold sweat of panic. Body-image focused self-sabotage is a major contributor to our feelings of discontentment, isolation and fear. But, the best part about identifying one of our sabotaging patterns is we then get to choose again! And again, and again, and again.

BODY IMAGE AND FEMININITY

As a woman, you've spent your entire life being educated about and told what your body should look like, act like, and be like. You've been trained to only present yourself in the most flattering of ways, to always use makeup and clothing to cover your imperfections, and to judge other women for being too risky or loose with their bodies and sexuality. You likely hold a belief that your body is meant to be covered up when in the presence of impressionable males, that being whistled at while walking down the street is a desirable experience, and that any sagging, dimples, sun spots, cellulite, white hairs, or excessive fat is indescribably disgusting and to be avoided at all costs.

Have you ever chosen to turn off the light before having sex with your partner so he won't see the cellulite, rolls, or scars on your body, even though he's seen them a thousand times before? Have you ever put on a beautiful dress that you absolutely love and feel like a Goddess in, only to hang it back on the rack because it's too fitted, too sexy, too revealing? Or maybe you hung that dress back up because you know you'd never wear it in public for fear that you might eat an actual meal and bloat like a balloon? Have you ever created strategies to ensure that you are seen as powerful (but not too strong) and relatable (but not too vulnerable) as you step into a boardroom full of your male colleagues? Have you ever avoided going to a yoga or fitness class because you feel unfit and don't want to embarrass yourself in front of all the "fit" people? Have you ever noticed that a friend spent money on Botox, microblading, laser hair removal, or some other form of physical adjustment and felt immediate rage, judgment, and annoyance at her decision? Or maybe even guilt that she's willing to spend that kind of money on herself and you aren't?

Don't worry, I'm not judging you. I answer YES to all these questions. And chances are that you, too, are nodding your head in agreement. You're welcome, Goddess. I see you; I feel you; I honor you. I mean, how could we not answer yes to these scenarios? Think about it. Every single day we are bombarded with 4,000 to 10,000 advertisements telling us how to live our lives. We are told what fragrance or perfumes to wear, how to care for our delicate underarm skin, what movies to watch, who we should vote for, what we should eat, drink, and wear, and how to lose that extra weight so our spouses will find us attractive again.[1] Even if these ads aren't directly related to our body image, they subliminally trigger deep-rooted fears and self-conscious wounds that have been placed there from years of external influence, traumatic intimate relationships, over-sexualized television, and many others. I know you already know this, but

I doubt you've given it much thought in the last few years, so let's revisit how it all works for a second.

We see a stunning woman who we idolize and love, for instance, Jennifer Aniston, and she is promoting a specific brand of body cream. Even if we have a preferred brand, or even if we don't like using body cream, we are now subconsciously creating a belief that:

a. we need this cream
b. if we use it, we'll look more like Jen Aniston

This subconscious messaging is why most women's magazines are littered with ads for every kind of product under the sun being promoted by famous celebrities. And although we have no personal relationship with them, we know, like, and trust them, thanks to good ol' pop culture and credibility.

These ads primarily come from Fortune500 companies as they have the financial means to get their words and images in front of us from all angles. Here's another not-so-shocking fact: In 2019, the list of female CEOs in Fortune500 companies was 6.6 percent, leaving the remaining 93.4 percent of roles to men.[2]

This fact means that most daily advertisements you see (all 10,000+ of them) are either created or approved by men. Thus, we are deciding how we should look, feel, and live based on the desired view of men. OF MEN! While I know this may not be shocking or new information and that most of us know this already, I beg you to take a moment right now to notice how truly BIZARRE this is. How ridiculous is it that as a society we have allowed our decisions about our own bodies to be dictated by men? And, what's even more fascinating is that when I speak to my guy friends about women's bodies and what they truly desire, their response is usually focused on a more "natural" and "laid back" look. I've heard so many men tell me that they don't care about a woman's size, what they are attracted to is her confidence. They love seeing her in fitted clothing that shows off her curves and takes confidence to wear. They love seeing her relaxed and laughing, eating real food (not just a green salad with the dressing on the side), and having fun in the moment. When it comes to sex, the men I've spoken to absolutely love a woman who loves her body, regardless of the shape, size, dimples, wrinkles, stretch marks, you name it. A woman who loves her body and loves her life—this is the biggest turn on!

And it's not just men. Think of the women you idolize, are attracted to, and admire. Chances are it's not just their body or physical appearance that you love, it's how they show up *in* their bodies, in their own feminine power and magnetism.

And now, add a whole new brand of external pressure—the social media influencers. These are the women we have been following online for years. We love their content, we know their families, we feel like we are Insta-besties, which brings with it a high level of trust and impressionability. Some of these individuals receive compensation and/or are endorsed very generously to convince you that you need to own the same clothing, eat the same food, and stay at the same oceanside resorts as they do. These individuals are often making a tremendous amount of money on ONE sponsored post.

For the record, I am fully supportive of influencer marketing. To me, it is far more organic and natural than previous forms of marketing; however, it comes with its own set of boundaries. Remember that just because someone appears to be sharing "all" of their life on social media, they are still choosing and curating their feed strategically, especially if they are making six figures for doing so. Hence the phrase, *the highlight reel.*

Be conscious about how your internal dialogue interacts with your social media feeds. Can you truly trust someone you've never met or had a personal conversation with? And furthermore, are you sure that their personal taste in products is the same as yours? I've been caught wanting to buy specific types of makeup from a beauty blogger I accidentally stumbled upon late at night on YouTube, until I remembered that I prefer to buy local, organic, and environmentally friendly products, and she didn't mention any of those things at all. I was just drawn into the idea of having flawless makeup and looking like she did. Make sure you are curating your social media feed to represent your values and goals! And always consult your intuition before making a purchase, regardless of the sale price!

Yes, there is a fair amount of external pressure and stimuli that influences our internal dialogue daily, but let's get into the nitty-gritty of how it truly makes an impact on our lives.

Can you remember being a young teenager, starting to understand and enjoy the new womanly body you've developed and experimenting with attention-seeking actions?

Remember that the Feminine loves to seen, desired, and lusted after. Thus, these actions were a completely natural experience of growth and maturity.

Take a moment to journey back to this time in your life.

Remember the emotional highs, the curiosity, the focus on finding the most joy in any activity. Remember the feeling of coming into your womanhood, the first time you got your period, your first kiss, your first party with friends . . .

I remember a specific moment when I was young; I was in junior high school. It was summer, and the nights were long and hot—I loved it! I was on my way to a party, and my mom caught a glimpse of my short skirt and low-cut tank top and gave me the eye . . . the eye that said, "Deanna, you better go change before I MAKE you." To avoid the wrath of my mom, and because I was obsessed with being a "good girl" for my affection and attention, I obviously changed clothes. I put on something more modest: an outfit that didn't show off my lady lumps or curves or create any sex appeal with my body.

In this instance my mom was trying to protect me and ensure I had morals and values about my body when it came to the opposite sex, but what neither of us realized at the time was that from my mom's protective and understandable actions, I subconsciously ingrained this belief:

You can't trust men when it comes to sex;
therefore, always dress and act on the side
of caution as to not call too much sexual
attention to yourself.

I'm quite confident that you can relate to this belief: As a woman, it is our duty and job to ensure that we are safe from sexual exploitation by covering up our bodies, refraining from exposing ourselves in a sensual manner, and dulling down our Goddess-ness—yes, perhaps these actions will lead to fewer unwanted sexual experiences.

But have we even taken a moment to consider how backward this belief is?

That, as women, who are born with breasts and vaginas, it is *our job* to cover ourselves so the "poor and defenseless" opposite sex can restrain their uncontrollable lust toward a woman's body. And not only that, consider all the ways we try to cover up our "imperfect" bodies as adult women so our men, most of whom are long-term partners, will still find us attractive.

We hold the belief that women, in our
natural and purest form, are either too
powerful or too hideous. When it comes to
our bodies, we allow all our power to live in
the hands and the choices of the opposite
sex.

Wow!

Even just reading through my own words right now, my eyes have welled up with tears and there is a lump my throat. This is not right, ladies. This is not the way it is supposed to be. We are NOT too powerful, and we are certainly NOT hideous, and we do NOT need to be "fixed" or covered up, EVER!

Can we make a conscious decision together right now? Can we say NO to allowing this type of pressure to rule our lives? Even if that looks like wearing that tight dress although we're slightly insecure, or choosing to keep the lights on at night, or holding our tongue when we want to comment on our weight to our partner/kids/friends? Instead, we will take a few deep breaths and remind ourselves that we are BEAUTIFUL. Can we make this pact together? I hope so. I'm holding the vision in my heart and my mind that one day we will dance in the sunset's golden glow, fully embodied in our Goddess power, uninhibited by our doubts and worries, and truly embracing the magnificence of our beautiful bodies.

Now back to that memory from my teenage years . . . Yes, I quickly changed out of my skirt and low-cut top, and yes, it was valuable for me, a young and naïve girl, to understand how to honor my body without needing the sexualized attention from the boys in my grade. But what this experience also did was set me up for spending the majority of my adult life terrified of walking the streets in a skirt or high heels, terrified to show off my cleavage for fear that I would be judged as a slut and others would feel invited to interact with me as such. I was terrified that my own desire for pleasure or self-expression would be the one thing that caused me the deepest pain and trauma within my own body.

I was convinced that every man I saw would do anything to have sex with me. I thought that simply by being a woman, I was a target for exploitation, and that somehow, anything negative that ever happened to me in terms of sex or lust or desire or even sensual play was my fault. Everything was my fault. Any negative experience I had could be traced back to what I was wearing, how open I was in allowing myself to be with others, and how I had invited unwanted attention. Here I was, a teenager wanting to look and feel sexy as I was expressing this new feminine power I had, and I was shot down by my feminine mentor (my mom) who convinced me that modesty is best when it comes to being around men because they cannot be trusted.

It wasn't exactly an empowering experience. And to be honest, it doesn't feel good to reflect on it. I've shed a few tears while writing this segment. Sexual repression is something that I have prided myself on having for years. To me, I was disciplined and obedient, exactly what a "good girl" would be—exactly what a good girl *should* be. In the past few years of really diving deep into my spiritual and personal awakening, however, I've learned that our sexual energy, lust, and desire are integral parts of our own creative ability and self-expression. This exploration has allowed me to start reflecting on how my own beliefs of myself and others are casting a shadow on the wholeness of who I am.

I believed that my power lived in being modest and drawing no attention to myself—in being an "untouchable" and not allowing anyone to "have" me or my body at all costs. I believed that no man was to be trusted when it came to my body and that their desire was far stronger than my ability to stand up for myself and say no.

Whoa. Talk about emotional confusion. As a teenager who was very creative and experienced a lot of sexual energy flowing through my body, I *wanted* the attention. I *wanted* boys to desire me. I *wanted* to flaunt my sexual Goddess power. This was my feminine primal instinct—to be seen, to be acknowledged, to be desired. I was drunk on their desire for me. I was a sensitive little girl who always desired more love, affection, and attention than I had. I was constantly craving more, so when my body developed faster than the other girls in my grade, I loved the attention it brought me.

But I was also terrified that it would get me into trouble. I was terrified to *use* this power in intimate settings. Were men really so scary that I couldn't stand up for myself? Would I be taken advantage of at any moment, even if I said no? Was it really my fault that they desired me sexually? Was my body *my* responsibility to keep hidden so that it could be easier for *them* to keep their jollies to themselves?

Instead of looking for the truth, I shut up, hid my body, and pretended I didn't know that I possessed such a power within myself. I acted as though I was innocent and knew nothing of the opposite sex's lust and desire for me. And in time, it became true. Friends would tell me guys were interested in me, and I would genuinely be surprised. I had repressed the creative sensual power so deeply within me that I was totally out of alignment with what was actually happening in my life. It has taken me years to open myself back up to begin experiencing this energy. And I know I still have so far to go, as do we as a collective.

Please know that whether your beliefs support or deny what I'm sharing with you right now, your sexual energy is exactly that: it is creative energy. And energy is who and what we are. It is this energy that literally creates life. And if you're a mama, you know this fact. Your own sexual desire allowed your babies to come into this world. Start seeing your own body, desires, lust, and creativity as exactly that—energy that can transmute a desire or thought into something tangible and whole. You, as the woman that you are today, have that power. You have that strength. You have that ability. Regardless of being a mama or not, we all have this ability to use our Divine Feminine, our Goddess Shakti energy, to cultivate a life of beautiful and intimate healing and love.

Your body, exactly as it is right now, can cultivate this healing.

Your body, with all its scars, dimples, and wrinkles, can cultivate this healing.

Your body, whether it's forty pounds overweight or feeling far too skinny, can cultivate this healing.

Your body, right here, right now, in this moment, is MAGNIFICENT.

What would it feel to like to live and breathe as though you believed it to be true?

Dear Body,

I'm sorry.
I'm sorry for the way I've treated you over the years.
I'm sorry for the judgments, the hatred, the self-loathing.
I'm sorry for depriving you of food to lose weight.
I'm sorry for eating foods I know you hate.
I'm sorry for judging you for every lump and bump and mark and pimple.
I'm sorry for hiding you in the dark.

I'm sorry for not trusting you, for letting "their approval" be more important than my own.
I'm sorry for the pain I've inflicted on you.

Body, I'm sorry.
Please forgive me.

I am ready to begin again.
I am ready to choose love.
I am ready to honor you, to celebrate you, to witness your magnificence and beauty.
I promise to change my thinking.
I promise to change my words.
I promise to change my actions.
I promise to love you, more and more, with every passing day.

Dear Body, I love you.

OWNING YOUR BODY AND HEALING YOUR TRAUMA

We have addressed body image and we have addressed being unable to feel at home within our very beautiful feminine bodies. And the inability to feel at home within our own bodies, as women, stems from subscribing to a very masculine ideology of what is acceptable. Nonetheless, there is beauty in both masculine and feminine energy, when in sync. The problem arises when we are imbalanced or suppressing one over the other. When I look back at my experience in my teenage years, there were many positives that came from the upbringing I had. As with everything in life, every experience has both a dark and a light side. While it has taken me many years to awaken to my own power and strength, I am deeply grateful for the lessons and teachings that my mom and other mentors taught me at a young age because they helped me be cautious when it came to sexual adventures as a teenager. For instance:

- I said no enough times to a high school boyfriend who kept trying to touch my body when I didn't want him to (he dumped me the next day, and this is when I learned the necessity of exerting power behind my words).

- I dated my first love for an entire year before we had sex simply because I said so. I asserted myself and stated what I was comfortable with and what I wasn't, and he was respectful of my body and request. For that, I am so grateful.

- I went out dancing, flirting, and cultivating sex appeal with men on many occasions, only to leave without them because I preferred going home alone. I respected what I wanted and chose me over giving in to their pleas and advances.

I built personal strength and resiliency and gratefully attracted partners who respected my boundaries. I am honored to have had these experiences.

I also know that not all our stories are the same. For you, perhaps the Divine Feminine experience has been tainted by the aggressiveness and brutality of the wounded masculine. Or maybe you are choosing to numb out and either repress your sensuality or flaunt it in a manner that feels inauthentic to your heart.

Please, Goddess, know this: Your story, your current relationship with your own sensuality and pleasure is so valuable and essential to you embodying your feminine warrior. It is your journey, your experience, and your story. No one can ever take that away from you.

In this moment you get to choose how you desire to step forward into the next moment of your life:

If there is a part of your being that is craving support, guidance, and healing, are you willing to say *yes* to her now?

If you're craving a deeper intimate relationship with yourself but are constantly using the *exhaustion* self-sabotage excuse, are you willing to explore a solution?

If you desire more lust and passion with your current partner, are you willing to have a conscious conversation and genuinely listen to their needs and desires as well?

Important note: If this section brings up emotions, triggers, or memories of past traumas (sexual or otherwise), please reach out for support and do not suffer through those memories alone. You do not need to feel isolated in your healing journey.

For sexual trauma specifically, please reach out to your local:
- Sexual Assault Center
- Women's Center
- Victim Services
- Doctor
- Trauma-informed Therapists and Counselors

If you are in Canada, please contact:
Women Against Violence Against Women 24-Hour Crisis and Information Line:
604-255-6344
1-877-392-7583

My adolescent memories and teachings about sex and sexuality caused me to feel incredibly insecure when it came to anything related to sex, sensuality, physical empowerment, eroticism, my body, my desires (sexual and otherwise), and creating a balance between my masculine and feminine energy in relation to my own body and a partner's.

The deep "good girl" desire to be sexy in the traditional way I saw in the media, combined with not trusting men around my own sex appeal, created confusing and emotional seasons of life for me. Well, a *whole* life for me. This confusion wasn't just limited to my teenage years, and while I've made great strides in this area, my healing journey is far from over.

My entire life I've been living in a body that is outwardly seen as athletic, fit, and beautiful. I've had friends tell me they idolize my body or my overall look, men have shared their sexual interest in a variety of ways, and many others feel as if I "have it all" in terms of body and beauty. But that is only their view.

For years I struggled with not being fit enough to reach my own standards, while also being too fit so that I couldn't complain about it with friends and receive sympathy. I was stuck in this middle ground where I was seen as beautiful and perfect, yet I felt empty, ugly, and alone. It was as though even if my thighs were tight, my butt was perky, and my makeup was perfect, I still struggled to feel sexy or desirable or happy.

For instance, I covered up my body in fear that someone would see my teeny, tiny love handles, and I avoided eating too much when wearing a bikini so people wouldn't know how much my belly bloats from bread. If I didn't feel noticed or appreciated or desired, sex was the farthest thing from my mind, and instead, I'd instigate a fight with my partner to get some of that attention I so desperately craved. And when I wore an outfit that I thought was gorgeous and perfectly put together but didn't get enough positive response about, I felt depressed, unworthy, and useless. Something as small as not getting enough compliments (note: I said enough—I needed far more than one or two!) on an outfit was enough to send me spiraling into a dark place inside myself, a place where I was convinced I was a useless piece of garbage that no one wanted or needed around. *From a lack of attention, to feeling unworthy based on my belly bloat, to my strategic choice of clothing, it all affected me.* This was how deeply attached I had become to external approval and validation of my appearance. My self-love no longer mattered how I felt in my body—it was whether I was recognized and idolized for it that brought me contentment.

What I didn't know then that I know now is that whenever we seek approval from someone or something outside of ourselves, we are on the path to self-destruction (and, if we choose to accept it, spiritual awakening).

It was never "their" approval that I wanted; it was my own.

It was my own love of my body that I so desperately craved. I wanted to love me. I wanted to feel loved by me. I wanted approval from me. I wanted me—I just didn't know how to pick me.

If you resonate at all with how I used to interact with my body and others, I want you to know that there is no shame in having lived (or currently living) your life this way. This entire section focuses on all the external pressures we've been brought up with and how they influence our internal dialogue. So please, if you feel shame or guilt, take a deep breath and remind yourself that you being here, reading this book, and committing this time to your own self-development is already leading you down a new path. A path of awakening. A path of empowerment. A path of self-love so great like you've never experienced before.

There is no need for us to keep these secrets anymore. I'm tired of women, including me, feeling like the only way we can present ourselves to the world is when we are poised and polished and that any other version is not good enough. It's time to share your secrets with the world. Share your worries and doubts and fears because it is in these unapologetic shares and conversations that we collectively experience deep healing. In hearing our girlfriends, neighbors, and colleagues talk about their darkness and their shadows, we give ourselves permission to accept who we are with our darkness and shadows. It allows us to know that we are not alone and that our private thoughts are not isolated—in fact, we all experience these feelings. We begin to bring in the light. The more we can shine light on the shadow of our broken body-image beliefs and sexual dysmorphia, the more we, as individuals and a collective, heal.

Pause. Breathe. Reflect.

🖊 What would it feel like to love yourself, your whole self, unconditionally?

🖊 What would it feel like to have confidence and courage running through your veins because it comes from a place of love instead of judgment?

🖊 What would it feel like to know your body is powerful? It creates life and nurtures it, and it heals itself if you allow for healing to take place.

🖊 What are some actions you can take to continuously cultivate a sense of self-love, self-worth, and self-confidence? What are some things that make you feel worthy, loved, and confident?

Our body is so deeply intertwined with our self-worth, value, and appeal as a woman. Have you ever noticed how much more confident and powerful you feel after a vigorous workout? Or when you've just shaved your legs or gotten a manicure? Our physical being is a direct reflection of our sense of self and confidence, which is why self-care is such a hot topic right now. When we pour our attention and energy into our own well-being and how we feel in our bodies, we feel better about ourselves as a whole. Whatever we think and believe BECOMES our reality, regardless if it's accurate or true. For example, think of a time when your husband or a friend said you looked hot in sweats and a topknot bun, but you didn't feel it or believe them. Therefore, in your reality, it wasn't true.

Throughout the last five years of coaching women, I've worked with amazing souls between the ages of fifteen to sixty-five, and not one of them is one hundred percent comfortable with her body. NOT ONE, regardless of her age, work, marital status, fitness level, or anything else. We women have been trained to feel inadequate when it comes to our bodies.

GIRL—LET'S CHANGE THIS!

How absurd is it when you take a step back and realize how idiotic it is? We judge ourselves constantly, all day, every day. And let's be honest, it IS an all-day experience. Seriously, think about it for a hot minute. How often do you:

1. Walk past a storefront and glance in the window to check out your shape?

2. Sit down at a café and then pull your pants up a bit higher to cover your stomach rolls?

3. Walk out of your bedroom for a dinner date and immediately ask your partner, "How do I look?"

NONE of these actions serve our greater purpose, none make us feel powerful and strong, and none cultivate self-acceptance. When we struggle to accept ourselves, you best believe we struggle with accepting others. And if we can't accept ourselves or others, life becomes incredibly challenging to navigate on a day-to-day basis.

I used to believe that no one would want me, trust me, or hire me as their coach if I wasn't always perfect. I thought that I needed to always wear the same makeup, have my hair done, have perfectly pouty lips, and speak in a professional manner in order to be taken seriously. As a result, this meant that 90 percent of the time I was unwilling to show up for my community; 90 percent of the time I felt "not good enough" to offer value or teachings or create content for my people; 90 percent of the time I felt unacceptable by the masses.

Ladies, I MADE THIS ALL UP IN MY HEAD!

I remember during my university years when I was obtaining my marketing degree, my fellow Commerce buddies and I would travel to conferences to compete with other schools through case studies. It was a well-known expectation that we would wear the most incredible pantsuit and jacket combos in order to *look the part*.

All throughout my teenage years and early twenties I always felt I was required to *look* the part in order to *play* the part; the part being anything I was trying to embody at that time. But the truth was, and still is, I am enough, *regardless of what I wear, or know, or who I spend time with, or what my job is, or how often I eat Kraft Dinner*. I am enough.

And you, you're enough! Right now.

You, in your pjs on a Saturday afternoon. You, in your Sunday grubbies, having a beer on the deck. You, all red and sweaty during your far-too-challenging gym workout on January 2. You, on the bathroom floor, wishing and begging for the strength to make it through one more day . . .

THIS is YOU. And this is life. It's pure magic. And agonizing at the same time.

The duality of already being enough, having nothing to prove, and yet feeling and thinking and acting the opposite—this is what we experience, day in, day out.

I became exhausted of this daily grind of self-doubt, so I made a commitment. I chose to always show up authentically online and offline. Sometimes I'll show up on a video with pristine makeup and hair. Sometimes without. Sometimes you'll find me in a perfectly tidied well-lit room, while other times I'm running down a hill in ecstatic JOY.

I have chosen to use my social media platform as a place to share my truths rather than subconscious and culturally conditioned lies. Sometimes you'll find me dancing in my underwear on Instagram— sometimes in an overtly sensual way as I embody my inner Goddess power, and sometimes with deliberate movements to show off my jiggle. To accentuate my rolls. To prove that the way my body looks does not define me as a woman, as a business owner, as a human being. When I allow myself to dance this way, then post it on the Internet to be there *for eternity*, I feel *free*.

> *I highly recommend you view the "Dance Therapy" highlight tab on my Instagram and then challenge yourself to do the same, even if you delete it immediately after.*

I am finally taking the weight off my shoulders of feeling "not good enough," "not skinny enough," "not fit enough," and accepting who I am. I am declaring to the WORLD that I am okay as I am, exactly as I am, without any filters or the need to explain away why I'm having a "fat day."

Now, I know reading these words you're likely thinking, "Yah, Dea, that's great, but I'm not about to shake it on Instagram for everyone to see," and that's okay! You don't have to. But you *do* have to shake it. Honestly, one of the primary pieces of advice I give to every single client is to DANCE! We hold so much tension, stress, trauma, and emotion in the fascia tissue of our bodies, and when we shake it, when we dance, when we move our bodies out of *joy*, it allows some of that energy to be released. That's why you feel amazing after a yoga class—you released stored energy and emotions that weren't serving you any longer.

Dance in the living room.
Dance in your kitchen.
Dance in your underwear.
Dance with the kids.
Dance on your yoga mat.

Blow off steam.

Release past trauma.

Cultivate visceral self-acceptance.

It may seem silly (because it is), but the healing potential within this simple silly act is phenomenal. Trust me, give it a try. At some point in the near future you are likely to look down at your body and think to yourself, "I just wish . . ." or get home from work and feel so aggravated by the stupidity of others that you'll want to SCREAM. In these moments, go shake it off and dance it out. Put the tunes on and shake it! Literally, shake your booty so hard it hurts. Shimmy your tatas until you wish you were wearing a sports bra. Put your hands on your body and grab that flesh and feel the potency of your body. DANCE YOUR HEART OUT until you are panting and sweating and realize it's time to do some more cardio work because, girl, dancing is a *workout*!

And then, as the breath comes back to your lungs, as your heart rate begins to lower, as you start to soften into the post-dance bliss, put one hand on your heart and one hand on your belly and breathe in love, breathe in acceptance, breathe in peace and compassion and happiness. Breathe in every kind and loving word you wish someone would say to you. Breathe in every ounce of joy you believe to be possible for you in this body. Breathe in the Truth of who you are: a woman who is doing the absolute best she can and that is ENOUGH! Hold your body and tell yourself you are beautiful. Squeeze that softness around your midsection and honor it as a symbol of your strength and perseverance.

And then whisper these sweet nothings in your ear:

I am enough.

I am enough right now.

I will be enough tomorrow.

I was enough yesterday.

I've got this.

I've got me.

I am enough.

Now, let's circle back to the moment of "walking out of your bedroom for a dinner date and immediately asking your partner, 'How do I look?'"

Do you think your partner *enjoys* that question? Do you think you come across as confident, strong, empowered, and beautiful? The answer is an emphatic no. When we ask this question, we are embodying our fearful and insecure little girl who wishes someone would cuddle and hold her and tell her she's beautiful. So, if that's what you truly want, **GIVE IT TO YOURSELF!**

Whether it's solo, with a support person, or your partner. Be held. Be loved. Be swaddled. Be affirmed. Tell yourself you are B E A U T I F U L as many times as needed to begin to feel more confident, secure, and *EMPOWERED* in your own body. It's okay to ask for what you want and need from others, even if at first you feel embarrassed by it. And it's okay to give yourself what you want and need.

This realization has been one of the greatest perspective shifts of my life . . . the realization that I don't have to wait for anybody to validate me, that I actually can give myself what I want and need. It's so empowering to know that you can serve your own needs. And remember all that validation I said I needed before, the multiple compliments on my outfit and feeling desired by the opposite sex? Well, the more radical self-love I cultivate for myself, the more I serve my own needs—suddenly I don't need their approval or validation anymore. Suddenly I feel good enough on my own. #empoweredwoman

And know that it is absolutely okay and wonderful to be an empowered woman and *still* ask for love and approval from others.

Feeling good about ourselves translates into our relationships as well, which is another massive perspective shift that has changed not only my life but also my relationship with my husband! As a gender, we ladies have very high expectations of those who love us. They must know exactly what we need, when we need it. And if we have to ask for it—that's unacceptable!

You know what really transformed my relationship with my body and my husband? ASKING FOR WHAT I WANT. He is not a mind reader. Consider saying the following to your partner:

"Honey, I'm feeling a bit insecure in this dress because my stomach sticks out like this. Could you please remind me that I'm beautiful and that I am so much more than how my body looks?"

How much does that sentence trigger you?

Take a breath and ask yourself, "How do I feel when reading that and picturing myself saying something similar?"

I was absolutely resistant to the idea at first. It seems so ridiculous to have to ask specifically for what I want and to admit my insecurities and faults so blatantly. But the thing is, when you do it, you begin to heal. You begin to realize how self-defeating your inner thoughts actually are. You begin to realize how often you are seeking someone else's approval. And ultimately, especially when you're in the thick of this self-acceptance journey, you get what you want! You get that validation. You receive that approval. You feel loved, and wanted, and beautiful, and supported. It's like a whole new world. He speaks words that you want to hear. You get to be held in the way you deeply desire. You feel seen and your fears are acknowledged. You are given strength to move through them. **It. Is. Magic.**

So when it comes to moving through your body-shame tendencies, enlist support. Ask your girlfriends to disengage with you when you bring up how "fat" you feel. Buy clothes that you feel BEAUTIFUL in, not just what's "on trend" and not really suited for your body shape (hello, being short-waisted and wanting to wear high-rise bikini bottoms). Eat and exercise in a way that SERVES your body. Don't deprive or strive—honor and nourish! Spend time every single day looking into the mirror, into your own eyes, and feel the depth of your presence and strength and power. Every day. It's hard work, but it is one hundred percent worth it.

WARRIOR WISDOM:

EFT Tapping is a really powerful tool to use when shifting your thoughts and beliefs from body-shame to body-love! Learn how to use EFT Tapping in the final section of the book.

Put these concepts into action . . .

I want you to start observing how you speak to yourself about your body all day long. Start with just one day and keep a journal nearby or use a note in your phone. Record every thought you notice, regardless of whether it's positive or negative. It is essential to witness and become aware of your subconscious thoughts in order to rewrite the story of your life.

When you notice negative internal dialogue, take a moment to become present with yourself. Place your hands on your body, close your eyes, take a few deep breaths, and say thank you to your body. Thank you for the curves. Thank you for the scars. Thank you for the parts that don't work anymore. Thank you for the saggy bits. Thank you for the bigger bits.

Say thank you to every single part of your body, and stay here in gratitude until you feel that pain in your heart gently subside. This exercise may take anywhere from a few minutes to doing it hundreds of times. I promise you that it works, so please do yourself the honor of becoming present with yourself.

Once you've recorded a few days' worth of inner dialogue, begin looking for patterns and trends in your thoughts. Where are you most cruel to yourself about your body? What time of day are you more likely to think negative thoughts about the size of your stomach or the shape of your thighs? When during the day do you feel the most turned on in your body?

And remember to always remind yourself daily, even if you doubt it, that you *are* beautiful, powerful, strong, and magnificent. You ARE the Feminine Warrior.

SEXUAL REPRESSION AND BUILDING TRUST

I have a story to share that makes me feel vulnerable, yet I believe it is important to bring light to. I suspect you can relate to it, so I'm just going to dive right in. In 2019 I traveled to Calgary, Alberta, Canada, to attend a Tony Robbins and Rachel Hollis event. I went by myself and felt like an established businesswoman, making a trip to do my research into what creates a powerful speaker and learning from the bigwigs themselves. I chose to rent an Airbnb downtown in Chinatown. One evening I took myself out for dinner after the day's activities. I had a delicious vegan burger and a big delicious beer! I sat in the sun and just soaked in the goodness of my life. I felt amazing, empowered, powerful, beautiful, and proud of myself.

Shortly after, I began my walk back to my Airbnb, about fifteen blocks or so from where I had dinner. I was feeling quite elevated after a day at a personal development conference, something that always gets me feeling pretty damn sexy in my body. Anytime I commit to my own growth, whether physically, mentally, or spiritually, I always feel sexier and more turned on by life.

This is the Divine Feminine in her element!

I honestly can't remember what I was wearing, but I know it wasn't anything low cut or too tight or overtly sexy in any way. But I was feeling pretty sexy, so my energy was definitely exuding confidence. I noticed that I was receiving a lot of glances and head turns, and after only a few blocks, I started to feel uncomfortable and hyperaware of my aloneness while downtown in a city I didn't know very well.

As I walked past larger groups of men, I sped up my pace slightly. I turned my eyes downward to avoid holding eye contact, hopeful not to draw any additional attention to myself. I mentally reminded myself of where my phone was and counted the blocks left until I was at my destination. I crossed the street to avoid passing close by a group of men, only to cross back two blocks later. I was sweating profusely, even though the evening air was cool. I was scared.

Nothing happened. No one made a pass at me. I didn't get mugged. No one even tried to talk to me. And yet I was really uncomfortable with my femininity and my aloneness. This experience reminded me that we don't necessarily outgrow that aspect of holding fear in our hearts when we're alone in uncertain situations. I've never actually been accosted in a city setting, and yet that fear still runs so deep in me that it presents itself in a visceral response that I can't control.

Being a woman is a magical experience, and yet it can create such fear and anxiety in certain situations. I am embarrassed by my inability to be confident and secure in that situation last year. I would like to be able to say that if anything had occurred, I trusted that I would be able to take care of myself. But the truth is, I wasn't confident. I am still working on my own inner peace and strength, and this vulnerable experience in the city reminded me that there is always plenty of room to continue my inner growth.

Perhaps this is an experience you are familiar with as well? Maybe something similar occurred in your past? Or maybe you have a more recent experience like I do? I wholeheartedly believe that as women, we have been conditioned to live in fear, keep our guard up, watch our every step, mind our every word. I consider myself an empowered woman—confident in her sexuality, her sensuality, her strength, her power, and everything that makes up me. And yet, all it took was a different environment and a feeling of being alone in my feminine body to be reminded that perhaps, on my own, I am not safe.

In my own body, I am not safe.
As a woman, I am not safe.

I encourage you to consider acknowledging that these feelings are the cultural conditioning for most of us as Western women. We have been taught that we are the inferior sex because we are physically weaker and that men cannot control their hormones or penises. We have been taught that simply because we have a woman's body means we are a viable target for men to act on. We have been taught that we are always potential targets of sexual assault and bodily harm. Because of the body we were born into. Because we are women.

As I write this, I am filled with immense grief and sadness for the current state of the world. It is June 2020, and the world is experiencing powerful riots and protests of the #BlackLivesMatter movement against the systemic racism that has been present across the globe for centuries.

Wikipedia describes Black Lives Matter as a decentralized political and social movement advocating for nonviolent civil disobedience in protest against incidents of police brutality and all racially motivated violence against black people.

As I share with you the disturbing conditioning and challenges of being a woman, I am reminded that as a white Canadian woman, I have immense privilege over other women in North America.

Over the past few weeks I have learned so much about systemic racism in the USA. I was completely unaware of the incredibly high level of fear in a Black American's body when being pulled over by the police—their fear for their safety and their life simply because of the body they were born into. This level of hatred for other beings is disgusting and barbaric, and it is essential that we eradicate its existence. Inspired by this movement, I have made a commitment to deepen my awareness and understanding of these cultural challenges that are being faced by all people of color in North America and the world. I have committed to using my own social platforms to elevate the voices of women of color through my podcast, events, and online workshops.

My awareness of this movement comes primarily from individuals in the USA, but as I witness those south of the border defending their rights as a human being, I can't help but open my heart and my mind more deeply to those in my own neighborhood.

On my EMPOWERED Podcast, I recently interviewed a powerful author, speaker and Indigenous woman, Elaine Alec. Within a week of stumbling upon her Facebook profile page and reaching out to connect, I found myself on a Zoom call with tears welling up in my eyes and a fire burning in my heart.

Elaine shared with me the heart-wrenching reality of her life—that just a few weeks prior she had to explain to her young daughter why a person would yell racial slurs at her in the grocery store when she was with her grandma. She told her the devastating truth that some people will treat her differently because of her culture and skin. At the same time, she is trying to advocate for her daughter that her culture is to be celebrated, honored, and protected with love. A devastating duality.

I always believed that not seeing a person's skin color was the most anti-racist thing I could do, and now I understand how that is, in a sense, "white washing" all of us to be the same. I am committed to learning more about the current and past challenges of people of *color and am grateful to be alive in a time when this information and these stories are so accessible.*

Thank you to everyone who risked their lives to protest, to riot, to fuel this revolution. You are needed. You are loved. You are valued. Your life will ALWAYS matter.

I will not be writing more on this topic as it's not my voice that needs to be heard. There are an incredible number of online resources from women of color to support your ongoing education and awareness of systemic racism. Please do your due diligence, regardless of your race, and educate yourself.

In 2017 we saw the rise of the #MeToo movement across social media platforms everywhere. This movement stemmed from the need to raise awareness of the pervasiveness of sexual abuse and assault in our present society. What I learned from this movement is that sexual abuse and assault has been, and is still, a very real reality for many women. One of the most disturbing facts that came from this movement is that most sexual assault cases against women occur with family members or close community friends. These abusers are people who women trusted, felt safe with, and allowed into their own homes. These "trusted" family members and friends abused women's sexuality for their own disgusting pleasure.

Ladies, we are taught at a young age by our parents, by society, and by experiences that our sexuality is a magnet for unwanted attention and threats and abuse.

Is it any wonder why we struggle to be in touch with our own femininity or sensuality? And struggle to feel proud of our body and allow ourselves any such personal pleasure? It can require a great deal of comfort, safety, and ease for a woman to truly let down her guard and allow another person to touch or enter her body. Even if that person is her life partner, it can still require time, patience, and comfort for her to feel safe to be held. This, too, is a by-product of our societal conditioning.

If feeling sexy, empowered, and beautiful in your own body could possibly invite unwanted sexual attention or even abuse, of course you would associate your own sexuality and body with fear. Subconsciously, your body became a target that needed to be hidden and protected at all costs. Even when in a long-term relationship, this conditioning can be challenging to soften, as most of us are unaware of how deep these roots live in our psyche.

I once had a client who was desperate to lose weight. She was a single mom who was ready to feel beautiful in her body again. She had been overweight for years and was frustrated that she couldn't shed the pounds. She tried many different diets, she exercised as much as she could, and yet the scale never budged. A conversation about her weight came up in every one of our coaching sessions as it was her biggest point of inner agony. One day as we were exploring where this deep desire and need to lose weight came from, she had an epiphany. She held a deep-rooted fear that if she lost weight she would draw more attention from men, and she didn't trust herself to say no or stand up for her own boundaries when it came to men making sexual passes at her. She realized that her body was holding onto the weight to protect her from being sexually abused.

Can you feel how deep that fear ran for her?

And how powerful our bodies are at protecting us?

Her extra weight and inability to lose it was based solely on her lack of confidence or trust in her ability to be safe in a sexual setting. And I don't mean lack of confidence in terms of wearing a curve-hugging dress—I mean confidence in terms of her ability to be safe in a potentially traumatic experience.

Pause. Breathe. Reflect.

How has your body been protecting you? From what? From whom? How can you start taking the first step toward allowing yourself to feel whole again, trust yourself again, and feel at home, feel safe in your body?

Social conditioning is not just an inconvenience, it genuinely dictates how we live our lives. It is time we decide to take back our power and EMPOWER ourselves from the inside out. Honor your past traumas and welcome in the healing support and guidance to release the fears you harbor. Give yourself and your body permission to feel, to heal, to receive love and nourishment. Give your body and soul grace for all the times you repressed its voice, for all the times you told yourself you were less than, not enough, or too much. This voice does not come from you. It is made up of the emotional and energetic imprints of those around you and the experiences you've had. Share your stories with your sisters. Be proud of who you are and know that you are NOT just a sexual object, open to being objectified by your community. You are a FEMININE WARRIOR who knows her worth, honors her body, witnesses her magic, and is taking a stand for our daughters and sons to live in a world where every human being's body is theirs and theirs alone.

"I believe that your tragedies, your losses, your sorrows, your hurt happened for you, not to you. And I bless the thing that broke you down and cracked you open because the world needs you open."

~Rebecca Campbell, *Light is the New Black: A Guide to Answering Your Soul's Callings and Working Your Light*

Section Three

UNLEASHING YOUR INNER GODDESS

DYNAMIC EVOLUTION IN RELATIONSHIPS

One of the most valuable tools we have at our disposal as spiritual beings is our relationships. I've heard spiritual mentors say that Earth is our playground and we are here to explore, play, mess up, and learn. And relationships truly are the most intricate and powerful playground there ever could be!

I've been surprised to learn that one of the most powerful outcomes most of my clients experience is a far deeper connection and sense of fulfillment with their intimate partners. When I began my coaching business, I had no idea this would occur as a result of working with me. I have never seen myself as a relationships expert in any way; however, I have spent years of personal dedication to conscious communication and observing how relationships evolve over time. When a woman begins to feel empowered in her own needs, desires, and wants, the natural next step is to learn how to ask for it in a relationship. There is an art to communication with a loved one that is unique to every partnership, but one foundational pillar that exists within every healthy connection is, of course, understanding that the relationship is never static.

Did you grow up like me, spending your childhood years fantasizing about a Disney movie version of romance and love? The classic expectation that you'll meet your soul mate, fall in love, go through a slight trial or tribulation, then live happily ever after, madly in love. For many of us, this scenario was our indoctrination to what love is, or at least what society says it is supposed to be.

And for me, add in a happy family home where my parents chose to never argue or fight in front of us and generally seemed perfect all the time. Seriously, they only argued behind the door of their bedroom, which was respectful and kind to their daughters, but also helped me cultivate an assumption that adults don't fight. I genuinely believed that once you meet your soul mate, life is easy and fun; that once you fall in love, everything else falls into place and life is smooth sailin' with no rough seas. I figured that being an adult was WAY easier than being a kid. All I had to do was make it to adulthood and I'd get a job, marry my soul mate, have some kids, and *poof* *bliss ensues.* I just wanted to "get there" . . . to adulthood and love so that my life could finally be easier and less emotional. Hah!

As I'm sure you can imagine, my life experience has been far from the reality of this belief. I did meet my soul mate. We fell madly in love. We spent all our time together, laughing, playing, having sex, and exploring life and what it means to be alive. It was truly amazing.

We experienced life through each other's eyes and spent hours talking about personalities and patterns, space and spirituality. We explored it all together, and it was bliss.

Until it wasn't.
Until there were rumors he had cheated on me.
Until the rumors were true.

Until it happened again, and again, and again, and again, each time with an equally powerful apology and promise that it would never happen again. There were whispers of how beautiful and wonderful I am, with profuse grievance that he couldn't possibly understand what had taken over him, and reminders of how good we were together, how we could make it through anything, and that we were truly meant to be. I was so confused. I knew that his actions were wrong, but I also knew he was my soul mate and that we were supposed to end up together. And so I forgave him. Every. Stupid. Time.

As the years went on and the cheating continued, my self-worth, self-esteem, and self-love dwindled with every passing day. I started relying on his approval and admiration to feel any sense of worthiness of love. I needed him far more than I had ever needed anyone in my life. I was like a love leech, sucking any attention I could from him, constantly complaining when he abandoned me at parties and assuming that he didn't love me anymore when he didn't call. I became a shell of the young woman I was when I first met him, and I didn't even recognize myself anymore.

I'd love to say I woke up one morning to realize how awful I had been to myself. I'd love to say that I chose to leave him so I could find myself, but I can only speak the truth, and that is not my truth. The truth is that he ended it. He called off our relationship by saying that he simply "couldn't do it anymore." I was devastated. Heartbroken. Scared. Sad. Alone.

I remember crying for days and days and days. I could not understand why he would end it, and I was convinced he would come around. I thought if I could get fitter, look more beautiful, be more independent, anything, that he would love me again. I wanted him so badly. I needed him so badly. I felt the gut-wrenching anxiety and pain of grief, of loss, of cellular sadness, and I felt this way for the following two years. I went over our relationship in my head a billion times. I vowed never to be so needy again. I convinced myself that if I just got my head on straight, he would want me back. If I could just make sure we stayed in each other's lives, eventually it would happen. He was my soul mate. We were meant to be together. He was my everything. He gave me life.

The entire time I was grieving, I was blaming myself. Not because of his infidelity, deceit, or mistreatment of me, but for him leaving me. I blamed myself for being too soft, too vulnerable, too attached. I was convinced it was these actions that pushed him away. So I started hardening myself, making sure I didn't allow myself to be or feel vulnerable with anyone.

I started dating again and chose boyfriends like achievements: I got them hooked on me and then sent them packing. But this behavior was happening subconsciously. I didn't actually mean to hurt them or be so hard. I hated ending a relationship and even hated saying no to a second date, but I was on an inner subconscious mission to prove my strength, my power, my independence.

I met some really amazing men. During this time I enjoyed getting to know them and had a lot of fun dating. But when I started becoming too attached or vulnerable, something in me would shift, and it would happen instantaneously. One day I'd be having an incredible time with a new guy in my life, and the next day he would give me a hug and my whole body would shudder. Nothing about him had changed, it was always me. I had become too vulnerable, I had opened my heart too much, and my body was protecting me from the agonizing pain of another heartache. It was terrible. I would "get over" a guy in an instant and have no remorse for how I treated him or how he felt when I ended our budding romance. Sometimes I didn't even call them to tell them we were done. It was a rough season for the men in my life.

I did have one partner with whom I struggled to let go. He was a wonderful friend of mine for years, and we really were so good together. We made a great couple—the infatuation and connection were real. But when that day arrived when my body shuddered yet again, I knew I had to end it. It broke my heart to hurt his. While I cared deeply for him as a friend (and still do), at that point in my life I was only looking out for number one. This breakup was the turning point for me. It hit me in waves: soft at first and then like agonizing yet angry waves lapping the shorelines of my heart. I started to realize that my attitude wasn't right. It wasn't me. It was a broken and hurting version of me. I didn't know these words at the time, but I was deeply embodied in my wounded feminine. I knew that unless I actively took ownership of my choices and healed my heart and tended to my whole self, this vicious and toxic cycle would continue forever. So I swore off men for a while and just focused on being me. I spent time with friends, partying, dancing, laughing, drinking, being the carefree twenty-something-year-old I was meant to be.

Throughout this time, while I continued to navigate the grief and loss of my soul mate, I became great friends with someone. He was kind, patient, fun, driven, and pretty damn hot. We had a strong physical attraction at first, but I had a sense that if I explored it at all, I would end up hurting him, just like I did all other men in my life. So I chose to say no.

We remained friends and hung out in the same social circle, going on camping trips and to music festivals together. The attraction between us never went away; I knew he wanted to be with me, and I also knew I held the power. It was my ultimate power play: I held all the power in our friendship, and it was up to me if I allowed us to get close or not. I was drunk with power. I loved it. Until one day, he called me out. He showed his strength and his power and forced me to make a decision.

I had meant to be en route to visit a previous lover for the weekend and asked this friend to drive me to the ferry. I purposely omitted who I was going to see, seeing nothing wrong with the situation, but he found out. I had never seen this strong side of him because I had been too busy being the strength and power in our friendship.

I remember the moment fully. We were standing on my back deck, the afternoon sun warming our skin, and this incredible force of a man stood in his strength. He looked me in the eye and told me we were meant to be together, that I needed to make a decision, and that he would no longer settle for just "being my friend." I was taken aback by the whole experience and quite turned on as well.

I forgot how good it felt to be in my feminine energy and not be so focused on holding the power in a relationship. That day I chose him to be my man. I cancelled my plans to see my previous lover and spent the weekend with my new man. I tried to make light of it by saying, "If anything gets weird, we end it. So don't go falling in love with me or anything," and he openly accepted my terms. We were officially a couple.

This moment happened almost ten years ago. We are now a happily married couple who have spent the past ten years openly dedicated to our own expansion and growth, both individually and collectively.

I always assumed that due to my previous years of being cheated on, I would suffer from anxiety and worry with future partners. But this man—my husband—he lets me feel safe. I have never once worried that he would stray, and I can feel his love for me in every moment.

I thought my first boyfriend was my soul mate, but perhaps he was my twin flame—an intense and spiritually awakening connection that is doomed to end in destruction for the greater good of your soul's evolution. But my husband—he's my rock, my foundation, my support. He holds my heart and soul in an incredible love unlike any

I've known before. There's no drama, fewer extreme highs and lows, and more partnership, companionship, and unconditional love. We allow each other to be who we are, even though we are so different. And I know this is only possible because we both understand and live by the belief that relationships exist within dynamic evolution. We are constantly changing, growing, and expanding, both individually and collectively. Every day with us is completely different, even if it looks the same outwardly. We allow space to face our fears, to witness our patterns, and to communicate openly about who we are in comparison to who we desire to be. I never knew this kind of love existed. I never knew I could feel so content and safe to be myself with another human being.

And in this safety, in this sanctuary of love, I learned what it means to honor my man as a king: giving him space when he needs it and allowing him to share his dreams and passions on his terms instead of demanding them on mine. I observe his strengths and gifts and celebrate him thriving in his areas of expertise. I honor the role he plays in our family, and even though he doesn't need to hear it, I remind him daily of how grateful I am that he treats me like a queen.

This is my soul mate.
This is my conscious relationship.

This is two beings who come together in their wholeness to amplify each other's gifts and strengths and support each other in their blindsides.

It is partnership.

It is companionship.

It is choosing to do life together.

Every. Single. Day.

If I had never experienced the grief and loss of being so heartbroken by my ex, I don't believe I would have learned how to build my own internal strength and resiliency in the way that I did. I also don't know if my now-husband and I would have worked out had we said yes to each other right away. We both had a lot of growing up to do—me in my internal healing and him in finding his strength and power.

I no longer harbor any resentment or anger toward my ex for the choices he made and the way our relationship evolved and ended. I can see now it was an experience that made one of the largest impacts in my life. I was forced to come back home to myself, and in doing so, I was gifted with an incredible life partner who I can share my journey with—a partner who understands that relationships take constant work as they are dynamically evolving. There is never a moment of stagnation, even when there are multiple nights of wine and Netflix while binge watching a show. Our relationship may look the same on the outside each day, but inside, we are evolving and rising to our highest potential. It takes a daily recommitment to each other to allow that love to flourish and grow.

Pause. Breathe. Reflect.

- What has been your greatest lesson through your relationships thus far?

- Can you identify a time you resisted the idea that relationships are meant to be dynamic and evolving? What was the outcome of that resistance?

WARRIOR WISDOM:

If you find yourself in a sticky situation with your loved one and are spending more time annoyed than connected, give both the Energy-Release Technique and the Emotional Trigger Release Technique a try for a few weeks. These two resources are incredible at helping you physically release any stored energy in your body and shift your mindset to manifest more ease and connection. You can find these tools in the final section of the book.

RELEASE THE PRESSURE

Our culture indoctrinates young girls to become selfless women who care for everyone else before themselves. In doing so, we believe we will garner the admiration, love, and appreciation of everyone around us. We will live a good life, be supported by the Universe, and feel fulfilled and happy. And to be honest, I love this model. I truly believe that the world needs more individuals who are able and willing to support those around them and simply trust that in doing so they will be taken care of by the Divine.

However, there is a major piece missing in this little equation. What about exhaustion, burnout, fatigue, disconnection, and depression? How can a person continue to only care for others when they are falling apart, whether physically, mentally, or emotionally?

In Western culture, whenever we experience the above-mentioned symptoms, we head to our doctor to be fixed of our problem—medications to regulate our hormones, medications to numb out our pain, medications to suppress our appetite for deep fulfilling love. But for the vast majority of us, *THESE ARE NOT PROBLEMS THAT NEED TO BE FIXED EXTERNALLY.*

We feel depressed, broken, exhausted, and anxious because we are following a life-model that is not designed to support us. We are not taught to FILL ourselves first and then give of ourselves wholeheartedly. We are not taught how to release the effects of a deep emotional trauma from our bodies. We are not given the tools to move through anger and rage in a healthy way.

I had an experience during the global pandemic of 2020 when I felt exhausted, apathetic, uninterested, and utterly bored of my life. I was depressed. I knew it, and my husband knew it. And we both knew I was a high-functioning depressed woman. I exercised daily, I ate clean, I went for walks every day, I read. To the untrained eye (AKA anyone other than me or my husband), I was completely fine.

But what was occurring underneath that exterior was me trying to navigate my way through a time in history with heightened emotional fear in the Conscious Collective. As an empath, this navigation is *not easy*. And while I had been building my skills for years, it was still more than I could handle.

I remember going for a walk on the golf course near our home. It was not yet spring, so no one was on the course. I was walking with Dixie (my fur baby), and the sun was shining and the wind was nippy. I walked and walked and walked until it all just came pouring out of me:

"God, I don't think I'm okay."

I couldn't hold back the tears as I admitted this deep truth out loud:

"I think I need help. I don't think I can manage this on my own. I feel lost, I feel broken, I feel sad, I feel useless. I have lost belief in myself, and I don't even care. I don't even care that I don't believe in myself, and it scares me so much. Please, help me. Please, help me. Please."

I cried so hard that I had to sit down on the wet, mushy grass. Dixie sat beside me, holding space for me to have my emotional release. I would love to say that in that moment the clouds parted and God showed up like Mufasa in *The Lion King* and reminded me of my value, my worth, and my place in this world.

But that didn't happen. I just kept crying. I picked up my phone to call my dad, then realized that calling him in tears would likely send him into a panic, and I didn't want to place my emotions on anyone else. I felt terrible. So sad. So broken. So lost.

I sat there crying for some time. The sobs slowed into sniffles, and Dixie continued to sit by my side. I was probably there for forty-five minutes, finally hitting my emotional rock bottom and admitting to the Universe that I wasn't okay. Metaphorically on my hands and knees, I was asking for help, asking for guidance, asking for grace. And when nothing monumental happened, no big aha-light-bulb-flashing moment of clarity, I reluctantly got up and went home to my little quarantined family (we took in two teenagers during quarantine—wonderful, fun, incredible, and challenging all at once).

The tears didn't fall anymore that day; my eyes were dry. I asked my hubby for a glass of wine and sat in our sun-room and cuddled Dixie. I just allowed myself to be present to what felt true in that moment. I smoked some weed, drank another couple glasses of wine, and let myself be. I let go of trying to keep it all together and allowed the truth of how I felt to be present. It hurt, but I also felt relieved.

What happened in the next few days was incredible. I still didn't have any one specific profound moment of awakening, but I started to feel slightly better. It had been almost six weeks since I had seen my best friend. She lives only five minutes from my house, but we were very diligent about not seeing each other during the isolation lockdown to help curb the spread of COVID-19. The day after my breakdown, we both decided, "NOPE. I'm done, I need my friend."

And so we saw each other. We sat outside on her grass, watched her daughter play, watched our pups play, and talked about our emotions, our frustrations, our laundry, and everything else that makes us, us. We cried a little bit, we laughed a lot, and we connected. I felt absolutely GIDDY at the opportunity to see someone I loved so deeply. It ignited something in my heart.

Within the next few days I also had a deeply relaxing day of nothingness. Like for real, nothing. I watched Netflix in bed all day, ate everything I craved, went for the shortest, tiniest walks just to get some fresh air, and continued to let myself zone out while watching all the drama I could find in the Upper East Side (*Gossip Girl* on

Netflix for the win). I fully allowed myself to let go of chores, cook-ing, cleaning, productive reading, and working out. I let it ALL GO for that day.

And the day after, the morning after that full day of nothingness, I woke up inspired, alive, awakened, and joyful. I wrote in my gratitude journal about ALL the amazingness that I had to be grateful for. I sat with my laptop and wrote on my blog, wrote social media posts, wrote about how we can make it through this pandemic. And as the weeks continued, I came further and further out of my depression. In due time, I declared to my husband, "I'm back!" as I finally felt like myself again.

> **When we allow ourselves to completely release the pressure and anxiety that we have attached to ourselves, it creates space for our bodies and minds to release that which we no longer need. In this space we begin to welcome what we do need.**

I was deeply depressed, and it took me being willing to admit it to my greatest mentor—God—and to fully surrender to begin to step out of the darkness. I was able to walk my way through the shadow of my own fears to find my joy again. If I had continued to keep it to myself, to pretend I was fine, to hold it together, who knows how much longer it would have lasted?

Master the art of fitting out, instead of fitting in. Start embodying exactly what it is you desire in life, love, business, and more. We have a primal instinct deep with us that triggers the desire to belong to a community, to be a part of the whole, to be accepted and loved for who we are. Belonging is an incredibly beautiful trait, and it promotes so much connection and community. However, the shadow side of it is our willingness to change who we are in order to fit in.

Your relationship with yourself must ALWAYS be your number one priority because it is the one that impacts and affects all other relationships in your life.

You are the common denominator of every experience in your life.

If you are struggling in your intimate relationship, ask yourself where you are struggling with yourself. If you can't stand parenting lately, ask yourself where you've lost touch with your own needs. If all you want is solitude, ask yourself why you're not allowing yourself to have it.

Say it with me now: *I am the common denominator of every experience in my life.*

By honoring our own emotions and needs every day, we cultivate an environment of authentic connection. Instead of being there for others because we've been trained to in order to be a good person, or because we feel guilty if we don't, we offer our love and compassion from a place of wholeness and ease. This offering supports both ourselves and everyone else in our life. It is a mutually beneficial symbiotic relationship.

When we allow our own needs to be met in a healthy and conscious way, we allow ourselves the spaciousness to support, love, and nourish our people. We live with more patience, more peace, more creativity, and more joy, and don't think for one second that your kids and your partner (and even your neighbor) won't notice that shift. There's a reason for the saying, "Happy wife, happy life."

You, my dear, are the queen of your empire. And even queens break down. What makes them a queen is their willingness to surrender as deeply as required to build back up stronger and more resilient than ever before.

Our Conscious Collective is evolving toward a love triangle that includes a level of self-love and appreciation beyond our current comprehension. It demonstrates a way of being in life that is symbiotic with the needs of both our own selves and all of humanity. It allows for a way of living life that fuels your own body, mind, and spirit, while also fueling those around you AND those you haven't even met. For us to start living in this way, we must first understand and embody the belief that *it is okay to not be okay*. We must release the pressure we place on ourselves to be perfect and emotionally stable at all times. It is this realization that paves the way for us to give ourselves permission to nourish our minds, honor our bodies, and express our emotions. And in doing so, the giving to, caring for, and nourishing of others becomes effortless.

WARRIOR WISDOM:

Creating a daily ritual of gratitude is a powerful step toward releasing the external pressure that we place on ourselves. Writing, reading, speaking out loud, and thinking about all the ways life is working out wonderfully helps your mind recalibrate your thoughts to seek more peace and ease. If you feel constant pressure that life will crumble around you if you take a break from your daily duties, give this technique a try! Learn my unique Gratitude Practice technique in the final section of the book.

THE FEMININE SUPERPOWER

May 28, 2018

There is wisdom in the not knowing. A sense of calm in understanding the Truth. When we release our hold of the reigns, we allow spirit to take over. We feel a sense of freedom and trust like none other.

To find oneself is the eternal game. Like a game of hide and seek, first we hide, hiding our Truth deep among layers and sheaths, hiding away all connection to spirit. And then, over time, we feel compelled to seek, to explore further and deeper to find our True Self once again.

By honoring the role Spirit plays in our lives, by surrendering to the deep knowing and wisdom of God, we will find ourselves, find our Truths, and never feel alone or lost again.

xo
Dea

Western society does not support the notion that a person can make a decision purely based on an intuition or gut feeling rather than sound logic. It simply is not accepted as a viable option. It's not necessarily discounted all together—I've heard plenty of people talk about "their gut feeling" or how they "just knew" something wasn't right—but it is often a small piece of a bigger puzzle that comprises of research, hard work, and mental rationality.

However, the truth is that our rational thinking gets in the way of our true superpower: feminine creativity and intuition. It is in this state of being that we create solutions that are one hundred percent so far outside the box that these solutions came from a whole different store. These are the moments when we finally give up searching and go for a jog or a drive or out for dinner with friends and the answer comes to us, so clear and strong that we can't understand how we missed it for hours earlier.

THIS is our superpower.
We all possess it.
Yes, men do too.

But most of us simply ignore it or discount it as child's play.

Ladies, this is your SUPERPOWER! Your Shakti, your feminine strength, your guidance, your connection to the Divine.

I coached an amazing woman for almost a year. During this time I learned a lot about the way business works between this woman and her husband within their company. He holds the more masculine title and role of CEO, while she has no actual title and yet is an integral part of the growth and expansion of the business. Her role is to use her "crystals and stuff" to help decide whether to hire that person, or if it's the right move to merge with this company, or when it's time to let that person go. She uses her intuitive nature to determine what the right next step is energetically, then action is taken physically. But the fascinating part is that her work all occurs quietly and internally, so to the untrained eye, it looks like she is doing nothing. And she is so good at her role that her husband rarely makes any decisions without first consulting his wife's "superpower" to ensure it is in alignment with his thoughts.

Now let's be clear here. Through the lens of our masculine-energy-driven society, her role is deemed unnecessary. It is not tangible or measurable; therefore, it doesn't make sense. It doesn't fit into a box that can be seen, felt, or understood. But this couple is so dialed in with their natural strengths and gifts that it is this particular role that she plays that has contributed to their high level of success!

It took some time for her to become fully comfortable with her role—to see her natural gifts as true superpowers that make an IMPACT on the trajectory and success of their business and life. But she did come to embrace them fully. Viewing our intuition as a gift is where most of us are missing the mark. We are so caught up in trying to "make it" in this masculine world that we are unwilling to see a world where life could come with more ease and flow; a life where we don't have to WORK HARD to find success; a life where balancing our energy levels is more valuable to the long-term sustainable success of the company (or family or vision) than our output or productivity. Constantly being in "hustle mode" and only focusing on productivity in overdrive (cue heavy masculine energy) leads to burnout, dis-ease, excessive weight gain, depression, and anxiety. We are trying *so freaking hard* to follow the rules to find success and happiness and joy that we don't realize that this pursuit of happiness is actually the culprit that is causing our discontentment in the first place.

There is no one-size-fits-all recipe for success. Our desires for success are based on our subconscious beliefs, worries, and fears, all of which have been cultivated since we were young children and influenced by those we admire and have looked up to over the years. That's why those online courses you've bought for business growth that promise $10K months haven't worked for you—they're not individualized and personal. And that's why when you signed up for that direct marketing company you were full of hope and possibility that you would finally receive that additional $2,000 a month you've been wanting, but after a couple months of not seeing the results, you quit.

Most of us believe that if we had more money, we would be happy and feel successful. And you might be. That depends on your belief system and what success truly means to you. I've had years of making a lot of money, and years of making a little money. I've spent a lot of money on myself, and I've been frugal and cheap. And I've had varying degrees of contentment and fulfillment during this fluctuation of financial abundance. There has been no specific pattern. Even the first time that I started reaching my financial goals every month, I simply increased my spending. When I stopped reaching those goals a few months later, I suddenly found myself in deeper debt than I had ever been before. More money doesn't equate more happiness or success. It simply creates more of what you believe. And for me, I grew up with the belief that money is hard to come by, you should always save more than you spend, and that rich people are snobs. *These beliefs are the reason I couldn't keep hitting my monthly goals: as soon as I made more money, I subconsciously created problems to ensure I came back down to my comfort zone.*

Think of the last time you hit a milestone in your life. You got the promotion, you ran the half marathon, you completed that course. How long did you feel good? A few minutes? An hour? Half a day? It is guaranteed you worked your butt off to achieve that goal, and at the end of it, all you got was a measly half day of celebrating yourself before you moved on to "the next thing" to achieve. Do you see how unsustainable this behavior is? How it is a perpetual hamster-on-a-wheel situation where you are constantly striving for an outcome or an output or an achievement only to feel less satisfied because now you have to set your goal even higher?

We've got our mindset twisted, ladies. But don't worry. This book is already providing you with the tools, awareness, and secrets you're ready for to come back to YOU. To come back to learning what makes YOU happy, right here, right now, regardless of what goals you hit or milestones you achieve.

Intuition is your innate natural gift as a human being. It is your gut feeling, your guided instinct, your sixth sense. It is your soul's message to you, guiding and supporting you along your evolutionary path. It is your feminine wisdom. Knowing whether to take on a new project, to reach out to an old friend, or to wear that dress to dinner—your intuition is ALWAYS guiding you.

I've been asked so many times, *What does it mean to follow your gut or listen to your intuition?*

It simply means to take action based on an energetic feeling or pulsation rather than cognitive thought. Our thoughts are a reaction to an energetic feeling or pulsation, but we are so used to identifying with our thoughts that we've trained ourselves to hear the thought more loudly. But when you get really quiet and surrender to the space between your thoughts, you can feel that energetic pulsation—you can feel your intuition. For some, intuitive guidance comes as visions and visualization; for others, it's a deep knowing with no rationale behind it. Some receive intuition through sound, others through physical sensation. We ALL receive intuitive guidance, but the difference is whether we're attuned to witnessing it.

Now, back to our thoughts and feelings. Our minds are limited to that which we have seen, experienced, read, learned, and witnessed in life. If one has never experienced another culture other than their own, they are probably less likely to consider cultural differences when preparing an international meeting. As the saying goes, *you don't know what you don't know.*

However, our intuition is energetically connected to Universal wisdom at all times, allowing it to be all-knowing and all-encom-passing. Thus, some intuitive nudges simply don't make logical sense—they are based on a framework much larger and broader than our minds can fathom. They come from our soul.

Let's play! Grab your journal, take a few moments and allow yourself to dive into these questions:

- What is intuition in your own words?

- How do you receive intuitive guidance?

- Can you think of a time when you received intuitive guidance and didn't follow it—what was the outcome of that choice?

- Can you think of a time when you received intuitive guidance and you did follow it—what was the outcome of that choice?

- In your ideal reality, what does it feel like to live one hundred percent in alignment with your intuition?

WARRIOR WISDOM:

I know this topic can feel intimidating or overwhelming if you're new to intuition, so if that's you, be sure to check out the Additional Resources section for more support in this area.

"*Your playing small does not serve the world. There is nothing enlightened about shrinking so that other people won't feel insecure around you. We are all meant to shine, as children do.*"

~Marianne Williamson, *Return to Love:*
Reflections on the Principles of "A Course in Miracles"

Section Four

LIVING WITH SOUL

SOULFUL RESPONSIBILITY

It is our duty as a human being to take responsibility for who we are, the thoughts we have, the choices we make, and the actions we take. It is never anyone else's fault or job or role to manage what we *do*. And even deeper, who we chose to *be*. It's not the fault of our parents, our upbringing, our socioeconomic status, our partners, our children . . . it is OUR responsibility. While all these factors play an undeniable role in shaping who you are, the time is now to claim full responsibility for ALL of who you are in this stage of your awakening.

Owning this responsibility seems to be one of the most challenging concepts for us to adopt as a society. After all, we've spent decades convincing ourselves that the problem lies *out there*, and if only *they changed*, we could finally be happy.

I lived by these beliefs for years. And when I look back at the main difference between now and then, I was always miserable then. I felt righteous in my ability to blame others for my own hardships and pain. I was extremely good at judging others for their choices and convincing myself that if only they were more like me, both of our lives would be far better off.

I was so hard on others. I used that blame as a shield for the deep-seated judgment I held toward myself. I blamed my partners and my parents for my insecurities in love and trust. I blamed the economy and the cities I lived in for my inability to earn a high wage. I blamed society for teaching me that I wasn't good enough. I blamed the media for my own body-image issues. I blamed everyone and everything possible for my internal pain, when in actuality, it was my own *allowing* of these beliefs to persist that was perpetuating the problem within.

Know that your own awareness of the choices you make every day IS your invitation to either hope or fear. Every thought, every word you speak, and every action you take is a CHOICE leading you in the direction of hopefulness or deeper fear. Once you understand this concept and start living your life with this awareness, this concept of soulful responsibility becomes fluid. It becomes second nature. You learn the difference between your Ego (fear) and your love (hope).

I know that life is not always fluid, easy, and fun. I know we go through hard days, hard months, and hard seasons. I know it feels sometimes like the pain and challenge is never ending and has become a new normal in your life.

Heartbreaks, grief, global pandemics, and business failures are inevitable and inescapable.

But where you can build your own inner resilience and empower-ment is in understanding that the way you *respond* to a situation is *entirely up to you!*

The following is a simple and relatable example that I've used for years. So take a deep breath and truly receive the teachings behind it, because this kind of work truly is *that simple!*

Envision two women driving to work in the city. They both have to be at the office at a certain time for a meeting, and each take pride in being on time and deeply value their position at work. On this particular morning, they are both stuck in unforgiving traffic that will inevitably make them late.

One woman, let's call her Sarah, is having an anxiety attack about the traffic. She is anticipating how angry her boss will be, and she worries that everyone in the meeting will blame her for holding them up and setting their day off-course. Her thoughts are becoming so real for her that Sarah notices she is starting to sweat in her brand new shirt—and this one shows the sweat marks. She begins honking her horn and yelling at everyone to *GET OUT OF MY WAY PEOPLE! I'VE GOT SOMEWHERE TO BE!*

In the other car is Megan. Megan needs to be in the same meeting as Sarah with the same start time and network of people who will have their days disrupted by her showing up late. While she prefers to be on time, she knows that this traffic jam is abnormal, which means that something happened to have caused it. Hoping that it wasn't an accident, especially with a fatality, Megan decides to use this time to offer more love and peace into the world through her thoughts and intentions. She hopes that in doing so she will help support those in the other cars who are visibly getting angry and upset. She turns on her favorite mantra music, consciously begins to breathe deeply and fully, and quells any nerves that she feels arising about her inability to change the traffic jam. She visualizes her arrival at the office being one of peace and ease and acceptance. She trusts that her colleagues are intelligent enough to understand that she is not usually late and that this is a situation out of her control. Therefore, they will begin the meeting without her to respect each other's schedules and time.

Both Sarah and Megan arrive at the office at the same time. Sarah is visibly in a panic, fumbling to grab her bag out of the car, getting her jacket caught in the door as she slams it shut and almost breaking her ankle as she rushes to get into the building without notice for the icy conditions. Megan appears calm and collected. She takes a deep breath before exiting her car, having a moment of gratitude for her safe arrival to the office and silently thanking her team members for having patience and acceptance for her tardiness. Both ladies enter the meeting and business goes on as usual. Sarah takes an additional ten minutes to settle in and calm her breathing before she can actively participate in the meeting, while Megan, who arrived calm and centered, has already shared a powerful new solution to their problem that just came to her as she listened and observed.

These women had the exact same external situation occur: a traffic jam that led them to being late for a meeting. However, can you see how they each had entirely different experiences of this situation?

It is our individual responsibility to manage our internal landscape because it is what dictates our experience of life.

We will all face problems, challenges, and terrible situations in our lives. There are breakups and breakdowns, deaths of loved ones, global lockdowns, children who refuse to listen, endings of friendships, broken washing machines, and everything in between. But none of these external factors have *any ability* to make you unhappy. None! It is your *response* to them that creates your experience—that is where all your power lives: in your perception and response to external stimuli.

> **Personal responsibility from a <u>soulful</u> perspective means respect and love for the greater good of all. Our souls are our epicenter of love and Truth. When we choose to guide ourselves through life using the essence of our souls, we are choosing to respect and love all situations, circumstances, and people.**

That statement alone may be enough for you to enter into a frenzy of egocentric thoughts and frustration and blame toward me. *"That's not possible! How can I love everyone? What about the murderers? What about poverty? What about my ex-husband?!"*

Again, we come back to the truth that your internal landscape and perception of a situation or person is what *dictates your experience.* To respect and love all beings and circumstances does not mean that you agree with or condone their actions or will continue to perpetuate them. All it means is that you understand for this moment in time, this is what is occurring in life. It is happening externally to you. And the only thing you *can* control is how you respond to it internally.

Let's be honest. Has worrying about, creating anxiety around, or complaining about your ex-husband (or former best friend or frustrating sister-in-law) ever actually created a favorable outcome for you? Or has it simply added fuel to the fire in your mind that he is terrible, not to be trusted, and you will be forever angry and alone? Regardless of what his actions are, it is your *perception* and *response* to them that makes you feel angry and perpetuates the pain cycle.

It's not his actions, it's your *response to them.*

What would it feel like to find patience, peace, and forgiveness for his choices (even when you completely disagree with them) within your own heart? Would that not create a state of internal calm, possibly so much so that you notice a solution to your current problem that actually empowers you and requires less interaction with him? The key here is that when you are in a peaceful and soulfully responsible state, you are creating an experience of life that is congruent with your desired state of being.

One of my clients, let's call her June, struggled immensely with her ex-husband. She told me all the ways he was a liar, a cheat, and an unreliable father. She had a few examples of situational proof as to why all her accusations were true. She was miserable, constantly agitated, and desperate for a change. Then during one of our sessions, June shared about a coworker who really got under her skin. This woman seemed to agitate her in every way. June was annoyed by the way she dressed, by the food she ate, by the way she slacked off and barely completed her work, and by her incessant need to talk about the most unnecessary things instead of getting things done. In this particular coaching session, June shared that she had just found out that her boss asked them to share an office space, and June was feeling anxious about it. We spent the hour dissecting the emotional response and where it might be coming from when June realized that this woman triggered her in an almost identical way as her ex-husband. The things she did were different, but the triggered sensations in June were exactly the same: anger, rage, annoyance, frustration, and loathing.

We decided to use external stimulation to experiment on June's internal ability to cultivate peace with her coworker and eventually, her ex-husband. In a short period of time, June was able to effectively release her anxiety and triggers for her colleague's actions and come to a place of neutrality and peace. And guess what happened next . . .

June's experience with her ex-husband changed completely. She was no longer walking on eggshells. She was calmer, more patient, and less emotionally attached to his words and actions, even though he hadn't changed at all. She cultivated an internal peace that was unaffected by external stimuli, allowing her more ease, grace, and joy in her life, even on days when she had to interact with her ex-husband.

Yay, June!

Remember, you hold the power to choose and dictate your experience of life. Every person and experience that triggers you is an opportunity to look deeper within yourself and cultivate a sense of healing and peace. This concept is seeing life working out FOR you as opposed to you being a victim to your own experiences.

Pause. Breathe. Reflect.

Let's put this concept to work. Grab your journal and explore these three questions:

- Where are you allowing an outside factor in your life (person or situation) to dictate how you feel?

- Why are these people or situations so triggering for you, and are you ready to release them?

- If these triggers disappeared, what would your experience feel like?

WARRIOR WISDOM:

The Emotional Trigger Release Technique that lives in your Embodiment Resource Guide at the back of this book is an incredible tool to use regularly if you live with intense daily triggers. It can be so easy to assume it's the other person's responsibility to stop triggering you, but this tool helps you to see the deeper meaning behind your triggers and what subconscious belief it's welcoming you to heal.

SOULFUL LEADERSHIP

When we commit to a path of inner empowerment, we often start by doing so for ourselves. We want more joy and less stress. We desire a healthier relationship. We want our bodies to be energized and full of vitality. We want more abundance, prosperity, and financial wealth. We want to sleep better, fear our boss less, feel confident in our skin, and experience more daily happiness than before. There is absolutely nothing wrong with these motives, but you need to notice how each of them are situated around YOU! Because, as we learned before, YOU are the common denominator of every experience in your life!

And here's why this initiation into inner empowerment benefits everyone else in your life: When we dive deep into ourselves and begin to experience the benefit of internal peace, we inevitably want others to experience the same. We want to share what we have learned and help others achieve their own inner peace. We begin to see other people suffering with the same challenges we once did, and we want to whisper the solution to them: *Go within; your answers are already there.*

I find sharing to be one of the most beautiful and intricate aspects of Universal energy. It's impossible for a human being to achieve inner greatness through the energetic quality of love and not have a desire to share it. Impossible! We are designed to suit up, show up, and serve.

Where most of us get tripped up is in believing that we must first give to others and then to ourselves. But when you study the laws of the Universe, sharing is not about giving from a depleted place. When we do, we walk away exhausted, drained, and begging for solace. The Universe is designed for you to give from a whole, inspired, and empowered place within yourself. Fuel yourself with love, compassion, gratitude, and joy so your cup runneth over, spilling out love, peace, and healing with little to no effort from you. This action is called soulful leadership—when your previously selfish motive of discovery turns to a self-full act of service.

I define soulful leadership as *respect and love for the greater good of ALL.* All! Not just you or your family or your community. For all humans. All beings. The entire planet. The entire Universe.

When you commit to changing your internal landscape to more peace, ease, and joy, you are energetically making an impact on ALL of humanity.

Remember the Conscious Collective? When you heal a past pattern that you inherited from your mother, you stop the cycle so your children will no longer inherit that similar belief.

When you heal a belief system of judgment or hatred to your own self, you are pouring healing energy into the entire Conscious Collective so others can heal that belief system with more flow and ease as well. This is how we create evolutionary change. It all begins with YOU!

Pause. Breathe. Reflect.

Start getting curious about your own inner dialogue around soulful leadership with these questions:

- What does the term *soulful* mean to you?

- In what ways are you already living as a soulful leader?

- Who do you admire that leads from their heart-centered soul? What about them inspires you?

SOFTNESS REVEALS STRENGTH

February 14, 2016

When asked how I feel, I respond, Yes!
Yes, I feel.
Yes, I hurt.
Yes, I cry.
Yes, I laugh.
I feel the pain of neighbors I've never met.
I share in the sorrow of souls long lost.
I ache for those who are seeking more but may never find it.
I yearn for love beyond what I allow myself to feel now.
And still, I am whole.
And still, I am me.
And still, I rise.

xo
Dea

I spent most of my childhood in bed, constantly sick with the common cold, flu, food poisoning, viral infections, ear infections, chronic headaches, and every other "little" illness you can imagine. It seemed normal. I was an active kid who happened to pick up bugs at school. Totally normal.

As I got older and my social life became more important, I realized that constantly being sick wasn't cutting it for me anymore. I didn't want to miss out on Friday night hangouts and weekend shopping, but I was still picking up a new ailment every month. I began to see my body as an annoyance—something that held me back from what I really wanted to be doing and forced me into what I didn't want: spending time alone with myself and my thoughts. This change occurred around the same time of my adolescence that my distorted body image became very prevalent.

I started seeing my body as a tool—something that either allowed me to fit in socially or be an outcast. Every time I turned down a social event due to being sick, I could just FEEL my friends become more and more annoyed. I was being labeled as *too sensitive*, and I was losing my social status (which, as we all know, is <u>everything</u> to a teenager). So each time I got sick, I started saying hateful things to my body:

"You're useless and annoying."
"Why can't you just be normal?"
"What do you want? Why are you so needy?"

I began personifying my body as an enemy, an entity outside of myself that was causing me disappointment and pain.

This inner dialogue continued for the rest of my teenage years and into my mid-twenties. I developed skills to mask my body's sensitivities, mainly using pain killers to push myself beyond my limits and paying for it in extreme agony later. I used this agony as a tool to stay in a victim mindset, asking everyone around me for support, love and to take care of me, because my poor, poor body was far too sensitive.

In my mid-twenties I decided to move to New Zealand for a year to travel and explore a new country. At the time I was working at a Chamber of Commerce as the Event Coordinator—a perfect "career" job for me, except I was *exhausted!*

I was paid well, I enjoyed the people I worked with, I loved planning and hosting events, but I was *so tired.* I remember asking my dad, "How do people ever have kids? I'm twenty-four years old, working full time in my career that I actually enjoy, and I'm exhausted every day!"

His response? "You just do, Dea; you just figure it out."

Well, that answer wasn't good enough for me. I've always been a bit *against the grain,* and I was determined to have some fun and get some energy back in my life before "settling" into my career and the things I was supposed to do: *get married, buy a house, and have a family.* So I set my sights on New Zealand. I don't know why I did as I had no prior connection to the little island country, and I knew nothing about it. But there was a feeling inside me that I was meant to be in New Zealand.

I made this decision around the same time I started dating my now-husband. At this point in our relationship he was an electrical apprentice, he went to school for a few months each year, he was in crazy amounts of debt, and honestly, he was a pretty immature mid-twenties guy . . . *but damn, he was good looking!* Meanwhile, I was a successful businesswoman, holding a well-paying office job, wearing sexy power suits to work, saving money for my trip with zero debt, and basically, just being a boss of my life.

Energetically, I was the alpha, he was a pup. I was teaching him about life, about money, about business, and it would appear that I was stable, mature, and amazing. When I asked him to join me on my trip to New Zealand, I didn't know what I was in for in terms of an energetic shift!

New Zealand is a fairly small country, and I assumed I would arrive there, share my healing and powerful words, create incredibly massive shifts in the communities and people of the small country, and that would be my life's purpose fulfilled. I know it sounds crazy, but please know that to me and my subconscious, it was one hundred percent accurate, possible, and true!

So, off we went to New Zealand to live and play for a year. The plan was to travel for the first few months until our money ran out, then settle somewhere, get awesome jobs, and just enjoy living in a different country. And the first few months were SO MUCH FUN! We did whatever we wanted, hopped in vehicles with new friends we met at hostels, drank too much beer by the beach, went out dancing every night, lived off white rice, carrots, and beans (a balanced traveler's meal, right?) and just loved life. *It was amazing.*

Then the time came to settle down and get jobs. We decided to stay in an adorable little surf town called Mount Maunganui. It was surrounded by sandy beaches on either side of the town with a big beautiful mountain at the core. There was amazing surfing, swimming, hiking, bike riding, all the things, and we loved it. We found an apartment with a couple from England and set out to find jobs.

Please recall that when I left Canada, I perceived myself as a successful businesswoman with a high-paying career and plenty of potential. So when I began sending out résumés to marketing agencies, community organizations, banks, and other businesses, I assumed I would have the pick of my choice for job offers. Guess what happened? No one wanted me. I got zero responses. I heard crickets. And I needed money after all my dancing and beer drinking, so I took a job with my new flatmate, cleaning rooms at a hotel. I viewed the job as a temporary interim one until I heard from my applications.

This job was *the worst*! My boss didn't bother to learn my name, and it was physical grunt work that caused my hands to dry out and be sore every day from the chemicals we were forced to use. I worked with some interesting characters who, while they fascinated me, were not my soul sisters and brothers. And the hours were unpredictable. One day we'd work for five hours, the next would be two, which meant I was barely making any money. As I continued to do the same repetitive work, I started feeling so incredibly broken, sad, and lost. It. Was. Hard. And, of course, I still hadn't heard back from any job applications, except for one: to manage a liquor store. It wasn't exactly the positive, inspiring role I had envisioned, but I went for it anyway. In the end they chose someone local since I am incapable of lying and couldn't get past the "How long are you in New Zealand for?" question without telling the truth.

This period of time was the beginning of the breakdown of my self-esteem. I continued on this journey for quite some time, barely making ends meet financially, waking up filled with dread about going to work, and feeling sorry for myself every day. Meanwhile, my lovely boyfriend, *the master of joy through simplicity*, managed to get a labor job at the dockyards. He made really great money, surfed after work, and was on cloud nine every day. Can you imagine the level of resentment that rose in me through this progression? We had completely swapped roles. I was now looking to him for guidance, support, and financial assistance. I didn't know it at the time, but this dependence was adding to my quickly approaching, deep and dark depression that would eventually cause us to end our trip. This depression became my reality of daily chronic pain, being so weak I couldn't leave the bed, excruciatingly painful migraines, and living off of boiled eggs and rice cakes.

Somewhere along our journey I had convinced myself that my relationship was the root of all my problems. It was my self-sabotage pattern of judging and blaming others playing out in full force. And he was the closest target. I had the belief that it couldn't possibly be me; you know, I went to yoga and stuff.

Even though I blamed our relationship for my pain, I was so insecure about myself that I was unable to leave him while still overseas. I was beyond broke, working at a hotel making beds and cleaning toilets for very little money, and I was homesick beyond words. I felt broken, alone, dependent on others, and so scared. I was constantly perpetuating the belief that everyone and everything was against me, and I unknowingly repeated these mantras daily:

It's hard for me to make money.
I am unwanted and unloved.
I am living in absolute paradise, yet I am depressed and in pain.
I must be unworthy of happiness or joy.

I was desperate for ANYTHING to bring me even a sliver of happiness. I spent my days in bed, too weak to do anything, grateful that I could see the beautiful Mount Maunganui through my window and drift off to a happier place in my dreams.

And then my body fully broke down. I became so ill that the only food I could stomach was boiled eggs and rice cakes. I couldn't leave my bed, and I had a twenty-four-hour pounding in my head unlike anything I had experienced before. I was deeply depressed, I was terrified to tell my boyfriend the truth, and I had no health insurance or money to pay for my doctors' visits and pills they kept prescribing. I was a HOT MESS! So we decided to cut our trip short and arrived back in Canada a month early due to my physical breakdown. Finally, I had health coverage, I had my dad and sister, and I had normalcy.

Upon returning home, being surrounded by support and family, and taking some time away from my relationship, something in me clicked. I started seeking answers to why my body was so broken. *Why was I the one who was always missing out due to being sick? Why was this such a pattern in my life? And how can I change it?*

I picked up the book *You Can Heal Your Life* by the late Louise Hay and started devouring every word. Suddenly it made sense. It had been my incessant daily thoughts of self-loathing and disgust that were attributing to my physical pain. Louise taught me that I have the power to change my thoughts, which would change my beliefs, which would change my life. *Oh my Goddess, YES!* My newfound awareness was blowing my mind!

> *"The thoughts you 'choose' to think create the experiences you have. If you believe that it is hard or difficult to change a habit or a thought, then your choice of this thought will make it true for you. If you would choose to think, 'It is becoming easier for me to make changes,' then your choice of this thought will make that true for you."*
>
> ~Louise L. Hay, You Can Heal Your Life

Take a moment right now to ponder that quote. How does your body feel as you read those words? What parts of your being are open to it being true, and what parts are feeling resistant? Allow all sensations to be present as you begin to expand your awareness into what is possible for you moving forward. How would it feel to believe, know, and trust that by changing your thoughts, you can change your reality? Feel free to pause here and journal on your reflections.

Slowly, with a lot of consistent self-care, education, and trying on new thoughts, I began to recover. I regained the weight I had lost, I developed a ravenous and healthy appetite, and I felt strength coursing through me. I felt energized with a renewed sense of purpose.

In this rebuilding, I began to see that my judgment and blame of my ailments on my relationship was a nasty self-sabotage pattern of mine. It took one month after arriving home to Canada and spending that month apart to remember how much I loved being with him. It took my own healing, my own journey of self-love, to truly witness how amazing of a man my partner was—and still is. I am eternally grateful for waking up to this Truth. This man, this incredible man, is now my husband and the one with whom I have chosen to share my entire life. That sneaky self-sabotage pattern was feeding me lies and untruths that almost cost me such deep incredible love.

It was at this time that I hired my first life coach, knowing nothing about the profession but feeling that it was right. My coach invited me to get very intimate with my own vulnerabilities. Up until that point in my life, I had always shied away from my own truths and fears by deflecting them onto someone else. I was a master deflector. It was always someone else's fault when I wasn't happy, satisfied, or content. But choosing to sit in quiet contemplation, reaching out and asking for support, journaling about my incessant worries, and becoming curious about my desires and bringing light to my needs allowed something within me to awaken. It allowed me to start seeing myself and my life from an outside perspective, something I now teach as the *Observer Mindset*. I was able to observe my pain and heartache and see the parts of it that were self-induced. I began to witness how my own choices perpetuated my victim mindset and caused such deep sadness in my life. I could finally see that in order to feel whole, I first had to fall apart.

It was through this acceptance of my own softness and my body's vulnerable breakdown that I began to rebuild my inner strength. I cultivated a sense of resiliency and confidence in myself, not just in my looks or my abilities, but in my trust of self to handle any situation. I began saying no when I wanted to and yes when it felt right. I learned about my intuition and started listening to that inner voice within me. I started truly living again, and it felt so damn good! Over time I began to see myself as a leader, as a teacher, and as a holder of space. I started to awaken to the Truth of myself—that I am a potent and powerful healer. I saw that it was my own resistance to my softness that kept my strength hidden for decades. As I began to awaken, seeing myself as someone with a message to share, I embarked on my journey of being of service to others. This journey was the beginning of my coaching business, hosting personal development workshops, giving spiritual talks, and cultivating an intimate community online. I was awake, living my true essence, leaving my mark on this world, contributing to society, and assisting in human evolution. My work became my purpose, and my purpose is my life!

Without my physical breakdown, I may never have connected to my Truth. I likely would have continued the pattern of physical breakdown due to emotional unrest and negative self-talk for another few decades until the pain became too unbearable. I am forever grateful for this experience because it led me to where I am and who I am today. Our strength comes from our softness.

When we lean into the softness of our feminine beings, when we honor our feelings and witness our body's requests and practice gentle connection to Self, our true inner strength emerges and unveils our superpower! It is our birthright and what our children, our families, and our communities are waiting for from us.

Enjoy this momentary experience of letting go, guided by the woman who changed my life, the late Louise Hay.

"As you read this, take a deep breath and, as you exhale, allow all the tension to leave your body. Let your scalp and your forehead and your face relax. Your head does not need to be tense in order for you to read. Let your tongue and your throat and your shoulders relax. You can hold a book with relaxed arms and hands. Do that now. Let your back and your abdomen and your pelvis relax. Let your breathing be at peace as you relax your legs and feet.

Is there a big change in your body since you began the previous paragraph? Notice how much you hold on. If you are doing it with your body, you are doing it with your mind. In this relaxed, comfortable position, say to yourself, 'I am willing to let go. I release. I let go. I release all tension. I release all fear. I release all anger. I release all guilt. I release all sadness. I let go of all old limitations. I let go, and I am at peace. I am at peace with myself. I am at peace with the process of life. I am safe.'"

~Louise L. Hay, *You Can Heal Your Life*

LEAN IN

I can tell that the patriarchy still pumps through my veins when I have moments of doing absolutely nothing and feel awful about it. I immediately jump to my to-do list: *maybe I should call my grandma; this is the perfect time to start those holiday cards; I should definitely get the laundry done.* These incessant thoughts pester me to the point that I can't relax into my nothingness; instead, am forced into doing more things. It's as though I am less of a person for being less productive, I am less worthy of abundance and prosperity, and I am less worthy of affection or love. Our whole society is focused on the concept of doing, achieving, producing, and creating. It's how we value ourselves and others based on what we produce (or at least how much effort we put in).

The following is a classic conversation between my dad and me:

"How are you today?"
"Good. Busy, really busy."

"That's great! Proud of you."
"Thanks, Dad."

The simple act of busyness is something worthy of pride. Our constant desire to be busy, even when it's not producing the results we want, at least allows us to sleep well at night knowing we tried our best. Except that we don't sleep well because we are overly exhausted and overly stimulated from doing too much, and we are stressed about whether or not all that doing will actually breed the results we crave.

It's extremely disheartening when you have the opportunity to simply be present, to be with yourself, to be with your emotions, to be with nature, to be with what is real in that moment, and yet our cultural conditioning pulls our attention away to:

"What should I be doing?"
"How can I fill my time?"
"What can I accomplish?"
"What can I do here?"
"What can I make happen?"

It absolutely strips us of the joy of being in the present moment. And in this present moment lives our FEMININE POWER! We are constantly analyzing what occurred in the past or strategizing for what we think may occur in the future. There becomes no presence—no awareness of the present moment.

Many people believe that the accomplishment of their goals is what brings them joy. And sometimes it does. Sometimes we do experience a sense of elevated joy from accomplishing a task. But how often does that joy last only for a fleeting second and then vanish so you can move on to your next goal? *What can I accomplish now? What's my next project? What am I moving toward?* It's as though the accomplishment of something is not even the goal but simply a by-product of our addiction to striving, pushing, and being busy.

When I began studying yoga, meditation, and spiritual concepts, I kept reading about the value of meditation. I didn't understand it because it was the opposite of what I was always told to do—it was literally doing nothing and just being. I was so resistant to it, assuming it only worked for a select few and the rest of us could find our happiness, contentment, and enlightenment from being busy. But with the highly sensitive body that I was gifted, I was never physically able to maintain an overly busy life for long before falling sick. It felt like such a curse for years, but now is one of my greatest blessings.

This addiction to busyness, mental stimulation, and productivity is robbing us of the opportunity to enjoy life.

To be in a state of joy, one must be in the present moment. Joy is a physiological and emotional experience, not a mental experience. So when you are spending all that time agonizing over a decision made in the past or fearing how you'll look in a bikini on the beach next week, you are not allowing the presence of joy in the current moment to be felt.

One of my greatest teachers in this realm is someone you may not expect: my sweet puppy dog, Dixie Green. (Check out her hashtag on Instagram #dixiegreen for all the cuteness you need.) This adorable fur baby reminds me multiple times a day to stop what I'm doing and simply be present. At first, I was annoyed with her gentle little whines and nudges against my leg. She would ask for my attention right when I was in the middle of something, and it triggered my need to be busy. But when I started viewing all experiences in life as a spiritual lesson, I began choosing to experience these moments differently. I began looking at her as a teacher, as a guide to a state of presence.

Dixie reads my energy well and often begins whimpering when I am getting frustrated with my email provider or annoyed at an incomplete Facebook graphic or irritated with how much I still have to accomplish. These are the perfect moments to pause, check myself, physically go to a different environment (often outside because, well, she is a dog), and reset my energy.

None of us are at our most productive or powerful when we are experiencing frustration or annoyance. Whatever you're working on literally becomes a waste of time and energy. I have found that with a simple reset to the present moment, I often return to the project with renewed energy, and a solution arrives shortly after.

We are not designed to be workhorses. We are designed to be intuitive, energetic beings that flow with the rhythms of life.

That upset stomach you have every morning after your coffee—have you ever paused and asked your body why that is occurring? Maybe even considered adjusting your morning routine to test out what may allow it to cease—or is that not an option because you have *too much to do*? Or how about that ache in your knee after an intense fitness class of weighted lunges and squats? Have you ever considered that maybe your joints don't love that intensity anymore? What about that nagging desire to go to the park or the beach and run around barefoot with your kids (without worrying about stepping in bird poop or on shells) and just have fun? Have you let yourself actually do that yet?

When you start leaning in and quieting down the mental chatter inside and around you, you begin noticing very subtle messages and guidance from your body and mind every day. It is these messages that come from your soul, your all-knowing Higher Self, that guide you to your deepest evolution. As you start to live in alignment with these messages, AKA your intuition, you enter a state called *flow*. Flow is when you are consistently in the present moment and can accomplish tasks and projects with ease. You are in your presence.

You are aligned with your greatest good.
You have activated your magic.

The more we wake up to the beauty of being in the present moment, the more we experience fulfillment from the inside, and in turn, experience peace from within instead of seeking it from outside of us. This transformation is not something that occurs overnight. It takes repetition, it takes conscious choice, and it takes dedication. It takes continually choosing a path of being and doing (instead of just doing). It is called *Inspired Action*. When your beingness inspires you to take an action, that action usually produces a much higher result or return than if you focused solely on doing. In other words, it is the key to doing less and experiencing more!

When I cut back my calendar availability for coaching clients, I had far more time to myself plus far more structured working time. Previously, I had one client on a Monday morning, one on a Wednesday afternoon, and a few group calls on Thursday around noon. Every day I had to be "on." But when **I restructured my week and allocated time to myself FIRST, it organically created a sense of fluidity within my days.** I created more time to simply be in the present moment—long, luxurious mornings of meditation, yoga, and nature walks, and being present in the evenings with my cooking, eating, and cuddling with my hubby. And I managed to get the same amount of work completed because it was done from my flow state.

I still experience moments of reverting to old patterning—that deep desire to just work my butt off from morning until night. As a creative, I find it challenging to identify my own boundaries. The work I do is highly creative, intuitive, and soul serving, and it is easy to overwork myself. So now, when all I want to do is more work, accomplish more, and check things off my list, I acknowledge that tendency about myself. I notice, with grace and compassion, my deep desire to be busy and productive for the goal of an external win, then I get myself out into nature. I sit down and I breathe. I notice the discomfort, I notice the fear, I notice the worry, and I notice all the emotions that arise from not doing anything by simply being.

It's not easy to be still and silent when all you want to do is be busy, but being still and silent is necessary to rewire your brain and reprogram your patterns.

Every time I am present with myself, if I allow myself to sit long enough in the being state, I walk away feeling renewed and refreshed. This practice is how we create new patterns: we acknowledge the old ones, choose to lean into the discomfort, then consciously decide how we want our lives to look and feel instead.

WARRIOR WISDOM:

If this concept of being in stillness and silence is new for you, be sure to spend time with the Breath Work and Meditation resources in the final section of this book. They will guide you to find your version of this inner connection.

The idea of *leaning in* is to not turn away. Yet in many instances we turn away from our fear, we turn away from our sadness, we turn away from our anger, we turn away from our worry, and we turn away from our actual dreams and desires because they don't align with our cultural conditioning. They don't align with what we are *supposed* to be doing and accomplishing. So we turn our backs. And what happens when we turn our backs is that the emotions and the experiences are still there, that discomfort is still there, and the more often we turn away from it, the stronger and more uncomfortable it becomes. Thus, we seek something to numb it. We seek something to make that feeling go away. I know you've heard of the common distractions: alcohol, marijuana, Netflix, etc. But what about the more subtle ones? What about diving into ANOTHER self-help book because you think this one is going to change your life? What about signing up for ANOTHER online course because surely you'll see this one to the end even though you haven't done so with the past ten that you've bought. Maybe you're getting into another negative relationship where you know that these patterns are just continuing and continuing but being alone with yourself is more uncomfortable than being with the pain of someone not treating you right. At least in that situation you can blame someone and run away from self-accountability and responsibility.

Other patterns include over exercising and controlling what we eat to the point that it's an unhealthy addiction. We're trying to control our physical makeup in a way that makes us feel important and powerful. And when we feel important and powerful, we don't have to feel our emotions, we don't have to feel the discomfort, and we can choose to suppress it by focusing on something else. Can you see what I'm saying here?

Leaning in is about opening your heart to the wholeness of who you are. And that wholeness, *I'm sorry to say*, is not pure joy every day. That wholeness is what makes you alive. We live in a world of duality—light and dark, day and night, summer and winter. And our culture tells us that dark and night and winter are scary, bad things. But how many times as a little girl did you have the best sleepover with your friends in the dark, giggling and laughing and staying up late and all you did was have fun? And how many times have you sat around a campfire late at night, looking up to the stars, seeing them all in the night sky, and noticing how magical this world is? And how many times have you appreciated, enjoyed, and absolutely loved the winter because it allows you to slow down, to calm down, to take time, and to be cozy inside with your family? It's our cultural conditioning that holds us back from actually appreciating the wholeness of who we are and this life that we live. *And that cultural conditioning can be changed.*

When you lean into the truth of who you are, when you lean into your wholeness, it will be uncomfortable, but what lives on the other side is a fulfillment and peace like you have never experienced before.

To believe yourself to be enough. To choose YOU every day. To honor how you are feeling without shame, without guilt, without fear, without suffering. Just honoring. Just acceptance. Just unconditional love. It's an unprecedented experience for most. We have not been taught these skills. We were not taught this in school, we were not taught this by our friends, we were not taught this at work. My loves, *this* is everything. And chances are you've read other self-help books, you've read other spiritual texts, you've read other books that are speaking a similar message with different words, *and that's perfect.*

I don't assume that anything in this book will be brand new to you because I know that you've already been exploring this information yourself. You'll notice that you've had mentors, teachers, leaders, and gurus who are all speaking the same message, just using a different dialect, a different tongue, or different words, and that's perfect. *These are the messages of life.* These messages are the spiritual guidance that you are seeking, that you require to embody that fulfillment from within. It starts with you leaning in. It starts with you trusting yourself enough to know that if you open your heart to your wholeness, you will come out of it okay. You will find your way to the other side. You will move through the darkness with grace and ease. You will know that you are supported enough, that you are loved enough, that you are worthy enough of witnessing your wholeness. I want nothing more than for you to experience this yourself. I want you to experience the vastness of your love and the vastness of your joy. I want you to experience life so fully that it moves you to tears and brings you to your knees in the moments of deep despair and in the moments of incredible joy.

This range of emotions is our gift as human beings. We need to stop squandering it. We need to stop pushing it down and instead acknowledge it for what it is.

A true gift.

When we lean into this gift, when we honor this gift, we begin our awakening process. We begin opening our eyes, opening our minds and opening our hearts to the Truth of this world, to the Truth of our life, to the Truth of why we're here.

LEAN IN. LEAN IN. LEAN IN.

"We have been given this precious human incarnation in which each and every one of us is a candidate for enlightenment."

~Michael Bernard Beckwith,
*Spiritual Liberation:
Fulfilling Your Soul's Potential*

ENERGETIC ALIGNMENT

Quantum physics and holistic medicine teach us that a human being is not just a body or just a mind. We are both. We are physical, emotional, mental, spiritual, AND energetic beings—information I was never taught in school. Nor did I hear about it at home. And it definitely wasn't spoken about in my peer group at any point until my mid-twenties. I did, however, have the privilege of learning about energy through Reiki healing from my aunt.

If you follow me online or have been to one of my events, you have definitely heard me speak of my aunt. My aunt is my incredible life mentor who I have always turned to for *all the things*, especially spirituality and energy work. She used to offer me *energy massages*, which weren't physical massages at all. She would run her hands along my energy body (hovering about three inches above my physical body) to move energy around and release any stagnation in my energy field. This technique was from her Reiki practice and where I began to learn about energy.

But this bizarre dynamic occurred in my life, and maybe you can relate as well. While Reiki made sense to me when I was with my aunt, no one else in my life believed in it, talked about it, or had experienced it. So it was this hidden experience that I was fully supportive of when with my aunt, but it just disappeared from my thoughts and conversations when I was everywhere else. I had such mixed understandings in my mind about whether this energy massage was a real thing.

Even though I was exposed to energy work at a young age with my aunt, I didn't start exploring it for myself until I was faced with my dark depression while living in New Zealand. It took my body physically breaking down, feeling completely isolated with my own negative inner dialogue and fleeing home to Canadian soil to finally start exploring *anything* to heal my body.

I started observing the words I said to myself in my head, choosing to fill myself with positive affirmations and kind, loving phrases. I envisioned the energy of each thought filling my body with healing, with love, with happiness and health. I began nourishing my mind and my heart from the inside out. Within about two months of being home and focusing on my inner self, my body was suddenly fine. I could eat again, I put on healthy weight, I had energy, and I finally started to feel *happy* again!

I used my love of fitness to dive deeper into the healing principles of yoga. Every time I exhaled through my downward dog I envisioned any energy that was harmful, hateful, and heavy flowing out through my heels into the Earth. I used my inhale to breathe in loving energy, healing energy, all the joy in the world. At first it felt a bit funny, but seeing the miraculous results occur in my own body made it much easier to stay committed.

This transformation was how I began to understand the value in my aunt's energy massages all those years ago, how our thoughts hold an energetic frequency, and that negative thoughts are energetically denser than positive thoughts.

I explored the Law of Attraction. I read a ridiculous number of books about energy healing and holistic health and alternative medicines. I started working at lululemon, a company renowned for their love of personal development and whole body health. My hunny and I moved into an apartment together and soon started looking to add to our family with our sweet little fur baby, Miss Dixie Green.

Year 2013 for the win!

Life felt balanced again, and I attribute it all to the understanding that we humans are made up entirely of energy. We can change and recreate ourselves in any moment as energy is in constant dynamic motion.

"...when our internal reference point is our spirit, our actions are motivated by love, and there is no waste of energy. Our energy multiplies, and the surplus energy we gather can be channeled to create anything we want, including unlimited wealth. When we harness the power of harmony and love, we use our energy creatively for the experience of affluence and evolution."

~Deepak Chopra, *The Seven Spiritual Laws of Success: A Practical Guide to the Fulfillment of Your Dreams*

Since my New Zealand depression, I have had many other moments and seasons of extreme physical pain and emotional depression, even ones that led to chronic vomiting and getting scopes into my stomach to ensure all was okay. And every time, physically (from a Western medicine perspective) I was completely fine. With each instance, once I focused on healing any emotional trauma that was present and changed the energetic frequency of my thoughts, the physical symptoms literally disappeared. Sometimes overnight. This physical pain is one of my body's gifts, even though for years it felt like a curse. It is my empathic nature, something I knew very little about for the majority of my life.

When I first began exploring holistic health, energy healing, and spirituality, I learned what an empath was—this description fit me to a T.

Empath: a person with the paranormal ability to apprehend the mental or emotional state of another individual.

While that definition comes from dictionary.com, in my own words, being an empath means to feel the energy of others—often emotions and pain—and to have an intuitive sense about another being. Empaths can feel the energy of humans, animals, plants, and even souls who have passed.

After learning that I was an empath, I began to wonder if all the pain I was accustomed to living with was actually due to my empathic nature. Perhaps it was my ability to perceive the emotional state and energy of another person that was causing me the constant agony and pain.

I have a vivid memory of being about thirteen or fourteen years old and hearing my dad and sister argue in the hallway right next to my room. Even though their argument had *nothing* to do with me, I couldn't help but sob and cry at the sound of their pain and anger. I just wanted them to be happy. I wanted there to be balance and harmony. I wanted the love and joy of our household to be restored. This was my empathic nature—picking up on their energy and equating it to my own. My aunt always said I was a peacekeeper, but in moments like that, my only way of keeping the peace was to feel their emotion so fully in my own body.

Over the years I've learned that being an empath doesn't have to mean that you are a slave to the emotions and energy of others. You can actually create energetic boundaries around yourself, choosing which energies to allow in and which ones to keep at a distance, all while still being compassionate and loving. It is this skill that enables me to do the deep healing work that I do with my clients. If I were still as open and sensitive as I was as a teenager without the tools that I know now, I would be absolutely broken and exhausted after one client session.

It's through my personal journey of physical pain and energy healing that I developed a method I use with clients called *Body Mapping*. It is an intuitive exploration of uncovering the wisdom behind your physical pain patterns in order to heal holistically instead of just masking the pain with painkillers and avoidance techniques. It illuminates the emotional imbalance behind a physical pain.

Empaths are often very sensitive and require different types of daily rituals and energetic support than the average person, which is why my coaching programs are uniquely designed to be sacred containers of energetic support. Whether you are an empath or not, the more attuned you become to your feminine energy, the more heightened your senses will become and the more unique energetic support you'll require.

WARRIOR WISDOM:

If you are a business owner who also identifies as an empath, please see Additional Resources for a special gift from my heart to yours.

I believe that most people are empathic by nature, and we can feel the energy of others to varying degrees. Some of us can feel it more deeply and have become attuned to the subtle frequencies of energy, and some of us are experts at denying our intuitive gifts in order to fit in with society. Wherever you land on this spectrum, I honor and bow to you, as you are showing up as the best version of you that you know how to be!

Think about how often people say *"you could cut the tension with a knife"* after walking into a room where there has been anger and fighting. Even if you can't see people with red faces or hear heavy breathing, you can still feel the energy in the room and know that something is off. This is your ability to feel the energy of another. We all have it, especially women. Women often have a heightened sense of empathic nature.

The great thing about working with energy is when you understand your own, you can learn to pick up on that of others, which is a powerful tool when it comes to managing the energetic environment in both a professional setting and a household setting. When we are so caught up in our own thoughts or fears or worries, we have no space in our minds to notice the energy that another person is expressing. Thus, we often miss out on the simple cues that we see in hindsight. Our energy is the precursor for igniting or defusing arguments.

Consider the following scenario:

Envision an experience where you are so caught up in your own fear and self-doubt around presenting your idea at work that you don't have the capacity or awareness to notice that your boss/ manager is having a terrible day. You simply go ahead with your presentation the way you planned it (and practiced ten times last night), and while it's a great presentation, your boss is not in a place to receive it because of the drama in her life at the moment. If you had been able to get out of your own fear and feel the energy of the other person and trust your heart to guide you, you likely would have asked a few questions first instead of bulldozing straight into what you need from her. The simple act of acknowledging someone else's feelings or state of being can be enough to help them become more present and actually hear what you have to say. Remember, just because you perceive someone else "higher up" than you in some ways, don't forget that we are all people, and we all have feelings and fears and worries and drama to deal with on a daily basis. Speak to the human in front of you, not the "boss."

Here's another example:

Let's say you desperately want your partner to pay more attention to you. You want him to tell you how beautiful you are, to notice those extra workouts you've been fitting in, to acknowledge the little things like your freshly shaved legs, but you just can't seem to get a peep out of him. You know he loves you, but the truth is that he rarely ever speaks his feelings out loud, and it's making you resentful and sad. Ask yourself, "Have I been in tune with his feelings or energy?" You have likely been so focused on how much he <u>doesn't</u> appreciate you that you are completely unaware that he is having an internal meltdown because of something that happened at work, or that the reason he's been staying up later and not going to bed with you is because he's struggling to make ends meet financially and is trying to find a way out of it before having to admit it to you. There may be any number of situations that are causing him internal grief. If you are completely unaware of his energy, you are completely unaware of how he is feeling, which is exactly the thing that you're *mad at him for doing to you. Can you see the irony here? Start by asking questions and trust your internal guidance when you observe a shift in energy or mood; it is a very powerful way to help others feel safe with and acknowledged by you. #consciouscommunication*

As Maya Angelou said, "I've learned that people will forget what you said, people will forget what you did, but people will never forget how you made them feel."

Energy and emotions are so intertwined, and emotions are just that—energy in motion. Our feelings, thoughts, words, and actions carry with them an energetic charge, which is what makes them powerful. The more we are attuned with our own energy and emotions, the better we are able to influence, make an impact, or even defuse the tension in a room.

Mastering our energy and emotions is what will allow us to have a fully human experience built on community, love, understanding, empathy, faith, and vulnerability—trusting that it is safe to be who we are, and it is safe to lay down our armor and simply BE.

In order to truly be present with our energy and intuition, we must master our emotional resiliency and mental clarity. It is these two constant human "struggles" that pull us away from our Truth. The *stories* of Ego—doubt and shame and judgment—that we subscribe to and allow to take up space in our minds are holding us back from expressing our soul gifts.

We are designed to live a life of purity—sharing our wisdom, gifts and intuitive nature with all. Until we are willing to fully commit to this as our *soulful responsibility,* humanity will continue to spiral in suffering, disillusion, and fear.

My dear Goddess, do not minimize the power of your Truth. Your energy, your intuition, your sacred soulful presence IS what the world needs. YOU are what the world is asking for right now.

Be brave.
Be bold.
Be resilient.
Be YOU!

MANIFESTATION

Maybe you've heard of a little something called manifestation? In its simplified form, it's the ability to actualize something you desire into your life. Manifestation is the feminine way of achieving goals—it's not about just taking a lot of strong, powerful action, it's about aligning your energy with what you desire and taking *inspired action* when it feels right.

Google tells us that manifestation is *an event, action, or object that clearly shows or embodies something, especially a theory or an abstract idea.* I don't know about you, but this definition does NOT excite me.

Manifesting, as written by Gabrielle Bernstein in her book *Super Attractor* is *"the creative process of aligning with the energy of the Universe to co-create an experience that elevates your spirit and the spirit of the world. Manifesting isn't about getting; it's about becoming. The more you let go, the more you become a match for what you desire."*

In my words it simply means *to create something from within*. To me, manifesting is *the art of connecting the energy of your thoughts with the energy of that which you desire to allow the Universe to co-create it into a physical form through you.*

In more esoteric terms, the source of all your desires (including money, relationships, opportunities, and things) is your consciousness of the Divinity within you *as* that source. It is your awareness of your own Divinity that creates what you desire to manifest on the physical plane.

You may have heard words before such as Higher Self, True Self, and God Self. These are all examples of your own Divinity. The Divine, Universal Energy, Spirit, and God are all names I use interchangeably when speaking about spirituality and manifestation.

When considering manifestation, I have many stories to share with you. Each one outlines what manifestation is and how it shows up in our everyday lives so clearly. But there is one story that keeps making itself known in my mind, and it takes me back to the fall of 2019 in a little ski town called Sun Peaks.

In November 2019 I hosted my first Empowered Woman Conference and was in complete awe of how easeful manifestation can be when paired with balancing masculine and feminine energy. It was an incredible in-person weekend that 80+ women experienced alongside me. Each woman walked away feeling inspired, ignited, on-purpose, and aligned with her inner confidence and empowered self. And on the business side, this event was very profitable! A fairly productive first conference, I'd say! Just one year prior, this entire conference was nothing more than a faint idea in my mind, but this is how we create physical experiences and manifest things, including money, from within. It all begins with a thought, aligning with the energetic frequency of that experience and then taking inspired action toward it.

Preparing for the Empowered Woman Conference truly took an entire year, but it wasn't difficult. I didn't work hard or suffer through the actions of planning. Instead, I allowed the ideas and decisions to flow to me. I spent time outdoors going for walks, practicing yoga, sitting by the lake, taking solo road trips, and meditating. These were the times that the most powerful ideas and problem-solving solutions came to me—not after three cups of coffee and spending ten hours at my desk. My ideas came from allowing myself to play and be present. They came to me when I created spaciousness within to receive the intuitive guidance. Instead of choosing to work *hard* on the planning of this event, I chose to *align energetically* with the experience I wanted my attendees to have. I spent time daydreaming and journaling about how I wanted them to *feel,* instead of researching events or working long hours to perfect the timeline. I deepened into my inner knowing and trust that the Universe would bring the right women into that room who were ready to receive my teachings. When it came to sponsorships and speakers, I didn't simply seek others who had the money to invest, I had lengthy and detailed conversations with each prospective speaker to express the *energy* with which this conference was being built on. These conversations allowed me to assess intuitively whether they would be a fit.

Of course, I also did the work. I created countless posts on social media for marketing, I spent time going over my outline, I had many,

many, *many* calls, I arranged beautiful décor, and I invested more money into my own coach to ensure I was energetically and emotionally supported. I certainly wasn't just sitting around only visualizing my event, and I also wasn't doing work for the sake of doing work. I was choosing to take *intentional* and *aligned action*. It was such a beautiful balance of masculine and feminine energy!

When the conference finally came to be, it was absolutely amazing. It blew my expectations out of the water. Each woman was fully present, open to explore her fears and worries even though it was uncomfortable. Their ability to receive all the teachings from me and the other speakers was incredible. Many of these women said it was the best conference they had ever been to, and from an organizer's perspective, the registration process was fluid and there were no major hiccups in the timeline or technology. I had aligned myself so powerfully with the vision of *love* and *transformation* that the Universe provided. I manifested an experience beyond my expectations, that served 80+ women (and a few amazing men) in a powerful way, and it all began with one simple thought. This experience demonstrates the difference between manifesting while in alignment with both our feminine and masculine energy and needing a specific outcome while living primarily in our masculine energy.

As we learned previously, most of us are stuck in a perpetual cycle of do more, make more, create more, have more, earn more. Masculine energy is constantly focused, it's always moving toward a goal, and it takes action in a very linear way. It's obsessed with living on the edge of death. Consider some of these common phrases:

"I killed that presentation."

"Work yourself to the bone."

"You'll sleep when you're dead."

These phrases are symbols of how addicted our society is to masculine energy. Many of us have become lost in assuming that the extreme masculine path is the only way. We have forgotten the strength, power, and creativity of our feminine energy: the power of play, the power of sensuality and softness, the power of creativity and daydreaming. We have forgotten what it is to simply *be* in each of those states.

When we live in balance with both energies—masculine and feminine—our actions feel effortless as they are aligned with our highest good. They come from an inspired and aligned place instead of forcing and pushing for a predetermined result.

When we're exploring manifestation, it is important to understand that we need to use both energy centers, not just one or the other.

When Rhonda Byrne's book *The Secret* first came out, I remember hearing someone say to me, "I read *The Secret*. All I have to do is think about being rich, and I'll be rich." I hadn't read it at that time, but I knew in my body that this belief was completely out of alignment with the Truth of the Universe. If what this person said was true, wouldn't we all be rich?

The piece that most people are missing when it comes to manifestation is that it's not just your thoughts that need to align with what you desire, it's your energetic frequency that must be in alignment.

This is *embodiment*.

For example, one time I wanted to receive $5,000 cash. I wrote it in my journal every day for a few weeks. I spent time breathing and meditating on the energy of that $5,000. I explored what it would feel like to receive it, how I would spend it, why I wanted it. It was so fun! I loved this experience.

I truly *embodied* the joy of receiving before I actually received in my physical reality.

And then one day, a family member showed up at our house, slapped a bank envelope on the kitchen table, and said, "You're welcome!" There was $5,000 cash on my kitchen table. I was AMAZED! But I didn't receive that money because I wrote it down daily. I didn't receive that money because I wanted it. **I received that money because I allowed my own energetic vibration to MATCH the energetic vibration of receiving $5,000 cash with ease.**

THIS is embodiment.
THIS is what manifestation is all about.

And this is a simplified story. Prior to that moment, I had spent hours and hours and hours in training, reading books, working with coaches, investing my money and time into myself and my study of spirituality, manifestation, and energy. If there is any part of you right now that feels the desire of "I want that," please notice the subtle afterthought of "and I want the quick-fix version of it."

There is no quick-fix version to manifestation, healing, or evolution.

However, when you dive deep into esoteric studies, you realize that miracles occur within a split second. Time is a human-made construct. The Universe, however, is not limited to any specific time, space, or dimension. The reason these miracles occur lives within your ability to align with the right energetic frequency. And how do we do that? *Practice!*

Meditation.
Breath work.
Journaling.
Releasing fears and doubts and worries.
Choosing beliefs that nourish our whole being.
Shadow Work.
Investing in an intuitive mentor.
All. The. Things.

When we are aligned energetically with that which we desire to experience, we manifest a life that opens our heart, expands our mind, and fuels our soul's purpose daily.

Manifestation and you . . .

What are your immediate objections and resistant thoughts to manifestation? What thoughts hold the energetic frequency of *no*?!

Look at those thoughts again. Are you willing to see through the lens of *possibility* instead of resistance?

If you were seeing through the lens of *possibility*, what would you desire to manifest in your life right now? Why? What is it about these manifestations that LIGHTS YOU UP? How would your life be full of JOY with these experiences existing in your reality? Let yourself play and daydream all the possible ways you can bring more joy, happiness, and love into your life through your soul's desires.

CONSCIOUS RELATIONSHIPS

There is a common joke between one of my soul sisters and me and it involves one of my darkest breakdowns and my ratty, old white bathrobe. We refer to it as the "white-robe moment," and it comes up often as a reminder to me when I am treading on dangerous Ego-focused territory.

In early 2017 I was becoming extremely fed up with my relationship. My partner and I had been together for quite a few years, had traveled the world, had gotten a puppy, and had moved to a small town to open our own businesses. We were fairly invested in each other's lives, and I wanted to get married. But he wasn't interested. In fact, he flat out told me we were highly unlikely to get married. I was studying spirituality and personal development nonstop and growing exponentially. He wasn't. I had big dreams, big goals, and a beautiful vision of being in a deeply committed, romantic, spiritually minded, and yoga-centered relationship with daily conscious discussion and being one hundred percent on the same page together. He didn't. When I looked at the reality of my life, we just weren't growing in the same direction together.

Something happens inside a person when they start understanding the depth of joy and love that can be experienced in a spiritual awakening. While I can't speak from experience, I would liken it to a similar experience as someone being born again in Christianity. The only thing you want to do is shout from the treetops, "THIS IS THE WAY!" You want to preach, you want to share, you want to teach and help everyone else experience the same level of happiness and bliss you've found within yourself. But as we all know, no one wants to be preached to when they haven't welcomed the information. It's wonderful when someone we love finds something that serves their heart, but that doesn't mean we are willing to drop everything in our lives and do exactly what they are doing. Instead, we love them and appreciate their journey from a distance.

This was how my partner was holding space for me. He let me do my thing, never questioned my esoteric aha's or channeling stories, and just let me be me. But I got so caught up in my head that he wasn't on the same spiritual growth path I was that the more I grew, the further apart we drifted. I had a tunnel-vision view that there were only two options:

1. I would become a deeply spiritual leader and be in a relationship that was unsatisfying and slowly crumbling while I tried to hold us together, or

2. We would end things and I would find myself a partner who was on the same page spiritually and emotionally—someone who was just like me.

I allowed these beliefs to grow for some time, slowly creating an energetic and emotional divide in my relationship. I sought out his faults and focused on all the ways he ignored me. I constantly noticed that he showed zero interest in what I was studying, and instead of saying something, I used this information as internal ammo and proof that our relationship was crumbling. I used my Ego mind and my tunnel vision to prove to myself that we were not meant to be together. It was breaking my heart, but it was the only thing I could think about. I was obsessed.

There was one day when I was in my well-worn, not-so-white-anymore robe with my hair a mess and a scowl on my face. One of my besties came over around 11:00 a.m. to check in on me. *She has this amazing spiritual gift of knowing when something is off energetically with everyone she loves and always manages to show up at just the right time!* I was so fed up with my relationship that I was ready to share my tunnel vision with another person. I told her all the ways he was failing me, all the things I wished for in a partner and how he would never measure up, and even worse, that he didn't seem to want to be this kind of partner.

I shared all my fears, all my worries, and all my dreams, and she listened intently. I felt like I'd created a captivated audience because she was eating up every word I shared. *Finally*, I thought to myself, *someone else can see how terrible my life is! And now that I have validation, I can actually do something about it.* When I finally stopped blabbering on about how terrible my relationship was, she didn't skip a beat and jumped right into a perspective shift for me. "You think you want to be with someone just like you? You want to be with a highly emotional, financially unstable, spiritually minded hippie who is likely to choose his own spiritual journey above you and flutter off to India without consulting you because he 'felt the urge?' You want to spend all day, every day, deep in discussion about consciousness and continuously be challenged on your own opinions and beliefs and held to such a high standard that there is never a moment of reprieve or 'normal humanness' in your life? You want to be with you? Are you kidding me? You need someone who is grounded, who is the opposite of you in a complementary way, someone who can let you be the star, let you be the seeker, the studier, while still having a stable home environment and safety of your family."

BOOM! Mic drop moment.

It was at this moment that I realized that his lack of interest in what I was studying may actually be a gift. I suddenly opened my perspective beyond my tunnel vision and was able to see that perhaps who I am meant to be with is the embodiment of a grounding rock energy—the Divine Masculine embodied in a man who knows how to work with his hands, stay down to earth, be one hundred percent committed and loyal, and be willing to worship me as a healer, a leader, and a queen.

Whoa! This realization changed everything for me.

In true Ego fashion, I didn't share any of these thoughts with my friend right away. I was likely trying to save face in that moment, but I knew something had changed. A shift had occurred, and I suddenly started envisioning myself dating me—how unstable that relationship would be; how uncertain I would be all the time about who would be doing the deep dive that day. Plus, who would keep us "afloat" in the humanness of our world?

I made a decision that day.

I decided to stop seeking proof that we were not meant to be together and instead seek proof that we WERE meant to be with each other. I started witnessing and valuing him for who he was instead of who I wanted him to grow into. I reminded myself that we all have our own journeys, and just because I saw mine as more important didn't make it so, and that just because I couldn't see his growth as exponentially as mine didn't mean he wasn't growing and evolving as a human being and a partner.

When I created this shift, I witnessed him change. While he wasn't attending the spiritual events I was, or reading the same books, or meditating daily, I noticed that he WAS growing spiritually in his own way. He was maturing and expanding his views of the world from our conversations, even if he wasn't initiating them. He was becoming more open to spiritual and evolutionary views, and I loved hearing his different perspective. We became more of a partnership than we had ever been before. It took me softening my gaze and seeing him in his wholeness, in his entirety, to bring our relationship back together.

Then, Christmas of 2017, my hunny proposed. I was in complete shock. I honestly had zero expectations that he would propose, and I had accepted that he never wanted to get married. But on that beautiful Christmas morning, him in a red Christmas onesie with a butt flap, surrounded by his dad, brother, and our fur baby Dixie, my man got down on one knee and asked me to be his wife, his partner for life. It was so magical. And so beautifully awkward. I truly believe it would not have happened if I hadn't opened my eyes to what was already there rather than seeking what wasn't.

It was in that white-robe moment that I was saved from ruining my relationship based on my own Ego beliefs; based on him not being "spiritual enough"; based on an idealized standard I had cultivated in my mind and could not let go of. This moment is why we need sisters, mentors, support, and coaches to help us along our journey; it is why some people feel as though they came into your life at the right time, because they did. Your soul contract with them orchestrated the entire moment for you to finally wake up to the Truth of your desires, which are always to live in, be in, and embody the essence of love.

When I reflect on how I was willing to end my relationship due to my partner not being "spiritual enough," I have to chuckle a bit. Every single spiritual text I've read and guru I've listened to shares that spirit is love and love is acceptance. I was using my previous patterns of judgment and avoidance to suppress what I truly desired—a deeply loving and expansive relationship, something I already had!

Spirituality is acceptance, an openness to finding the peace and joy in the wholeness of life and the wholeness of a person. It is not about seeking faults and flaws. It is not about judgment, standards, or requirements. It is about coming back to the essence of love within yourself and all beings around you every single day.

We have now been together for more than ten years. We had the most beautiful rainy day wedding on our three-and-a-half-acre property, surrounded by people we love dearly who danced with us until 3:00 a.m. We continue to consciously curate our relationship every day, creating space for each other's needs, growth, and fears. We argue and bicker, of course, but we choose to respect our own and each other's individual needs, desires, and dreams. We truly are a team, comprised of two whole individual beings, choosing each other every day.

It is from this relationship that I received the guidance to create a Conscious Relationships course. Many people have been through similar experiences, but not everyone has the cognitive awareness of what allows them to come back to a state of balance and neutrality. Living with conscious awareness of your relationships is an incredibly important part of your soulful responsibility, and I find it fascinating that this type of awareness is not taught in a traditional way.

There are two things that as a human being in a Western culture you will deal with daily: *money and people*. And yet, even with my Bachelor of Commerce degree, I was only required to take ONE personal finance course, which to be honest, was such a simplified course that it was the "easy" one of that semester. There is very little focus in traditional schooling on emotional intelligence, psychology, conscious social etiquette, or how to have healthy, thriving relationships with people.

Conscious relationships are not just focused on intimate relationships; it's designed for all interactions. I've attended and hosted enough personal development events to know that the average person has some beef (or marinated tofu for the vegans) with at least one family member. There's a reason that the majority of calls a police officer receives on a holiday weekend are for domestic violence.

We are not taught how to communicate effectively with people in our lives.

So, let's talk about it! What does it mean to have a conscious relationship? Google tells us that to be conscious means *aware of and responding to one's surroundings; awake, having knowledge of something; aware, painfully aware of and sensitive to.*

Relationship means *the way in which two or more concepts, objects, or people are connected, or the state of being connected, the way in which two or more people or groups regard and behave toward each other, an emotional and sexual association between two people.*

So technically, a conscious relationship could be classified as *awareness of connection.*

Most people have the connection part figured out. They know what it means to be connected and understand when the connection is good and when it's bad. What they are missing, however, is that awareness piece—the "conscious" piece.

In my white-robe moment, I was so focused on my connection with my partner being off that I didn't realize it was actually my lack of awareness that was causing my own pain. I felt disconnected, but I wasn't aware as to why, so I blamed him. (Can you see that pesky self-sabotage pattern of mine arising again?) That's why my tunnel vision and Ego started seeking external proof to create that awareness on my own terms. I wanted to control that experience at all costs, even though I was creating my own pain. I felt righteous and justified in my anger toward our relationship.

To be conscious truly means to be *willing to surrender*. You need to surrender your Ego, surrender your pride, and surrender your agenda in order to witness what is actually occurring—what is the Truth in every moment. You must surrender your need to control a situation and open to the magic of life unfolding as it's meant to.

When we surrender, we let go of our need to be "right" and instead witness what is true in the moment. In relationships, we are far more skilled at trying to be *right* than learning to *surrender* and trust the process and connection with the other person, thus leading to Ego-focused arguments about who's right, who's at fault, and a whole lot of disconnection. No one enjoys this disconnection, and yet we are so Ego-minded that we are willing to create discomfort via disconnection in order to prove we are *right* (even though the majority of the time we're probably not).

To be conscious in your relationships takes personal awareness of your role in each situation. For the longest time I was sad, frustrated, and annoyed that my big sister and I were not better friends. Ever since I was a little girl, all I wanted was to be her bestie, but that just wasn't how our relationship grew as kids, and this disconnect continued into our adult lives. Because I am such a sensitive soul, being with my sister was taxing and exhausting for me. I strived so hard to be who I thought she wanted me to be, but that persona wasn't true to my heart. We simply saw the world through completely different lenses.

My big sister is one of the strongest women I know. She is someone who, without a doubt, will drop whatever she is doing to show up for anyone she loves in a moment of need. I love this fact about her, and I am careful not to abuse it. As a highly sensitive and emotional young adult, I could have called her daily in tears while trying to understand the mess of my life, but I knew that that kind of dependence was far too much responsibility for one person, even for a loving big sister.

Early in my personal development journey, I decided to try an experiment. I wanted to see what would happen between my sister and me if I stopped engaging in the behaviors that caused friction in our relationship. So I stopped trying to *make her see things my way*, I stopped offering my unsolicited spiritual advice, and I stopped showing any deeply sensitive emotion while we were together. Instead, I chose to engage with conversations that felt good and ignore the rest. I gave myself ample space after our time together to process any emotions that arose.

I stopped trying to make her like me and instead started seeing her for who she was, in her wholeness. As soon as I did this, our relationship changed. There was far more peace between us, and we both seemed to breathe a deep sigh of relief. It was suddenly okay for us to each be our own person without needing to be like each other in any way. It created space to witness how similar we were in ways we had never seen before. It brought us far closer together and allowed our relationship to flourish.

To me, this change is everything! I love my sister so much, and I always have. To have a friendship with her now, like I never have before, is such a gift. The only reason it is present today is because of my willingness to surrender my own pride and Ego.

I was willing to become aware of what wasn't working for us and create space for what WAS working. I swallowed my own pride and was willing to show up in the relationship in a way that honored both her wholeness and her views while respecting my own, even if they were different. I allowed my triggers to rise and fall without taking action on them. I honored my emotions in my own sacred space instead of publicly. This beautiful friendship may not have happened without me taking personal responsibility instead of assuming it was her job to fix our relationship.

I am eternally grateful for this transformation in our relationship.

Our connection to those we love is *everything*. And yet so many human beings are living with hate in their heart toward people who have wronged them or hurt them in the past.

This trauma, this hate in your heart, it is a part of your journey for a reason. Your soul's evolution is guiding you to experience a healing of this trauma within yourself.

Are you willing to explore what that healing could be?
Are you willing to get curious about what releasing attachment to your Ego in that specific relationship might feel like?
Are you willing to forgive their actions in order to heal yourself?

"The practice of forgiveness is our most important contribution to the healing of the world."

~Marianne Williamson, Return to Love:
Reflections on the Principles of "A Course in Miracles"

Human beings live so deeply entitled about who we are and what we deserve from everything and everyone else that it is perceived as a weakness to even *consider* adjusting ourselves for another person. But what if it is this deep inner awareness and conscious choice to show up with compassion and humility that truly holds the power to heal the world? What if releasing our attachment to Ego and instead choosing to be curious and open-minded in all our relationships could bring us the most incredible level of joy, fulfillment, and peace we've ever imagined?

I believe it can. And my thoughts create my reality. Therefore, it is true. How about you?

You likely have some contrasting thoughts flowing through your mind right now, and that is perfectly okay. You're not reading this book to adopt every one of my beliefs and teachings, you're reading it to awaken your inner Truth and innate power.

Consider this: Your views and beliefs of the world are cultivated through your own inner perspective. Remember the example of Sarah and Megan who had the same external situation but had completely different experiences of it due to their inner perspectives? It is the same for our views and beliefs; none of us are *right* or *wrong*, we are simply who we are because of our perspectives. And the most powerful way to open your mind and body to a new perspective is to stop trying to control someone else's choices and views in life. When you release the pride of your perspective and open yourself to seek the similarities between you and another, rather than the differences, you open your heart to love.

In my willingness to practice conscious relationships with my sister, I was able to cultivate a deeper and very meaningful relationship. As a very sensitive empath, I had to learn how to practice emotional resiliency to avoid letting every difference of opinion we had hurt me. By cultivating my own inner sacred space for emotional release, I allowed myself to open more fully to connection with someone I love: my beautiful big sister.

To my sensitive sisters, honor the emotions that arise within you in the safety and comfort of your own inner sanctuary. This practice doesn't need to occur publicly. It can occur in moments of solitude while sipping your morning coffee, or in moments of deep surrender such as sobbing in the shower, sitting in quiet reflection by yourself, or even during meditation.

In these moments of sacred release you realize that we are all human. You come home to your connection to all. You remember that we are all made of love, stardust, kindness, and a whole lotta bumps and bruises, thanks to our very human experience of life.

The best thing we can do for one another, including ourselves, is release any and all expectations, stay open to new perspectives, love one another the way we desire to be loved, and see each other as the light that we are.

Section Five

EMBODIMENT

Committing to your own personal growth and expansion is not a gentle and easy feat. It takes dedication, commitment, and an ability to be with the discomfort of growth. Remember the show called *Growing Pains* from the eighties? There's a reason that growth and pain are often linked together. BUT! You've made it this far in the book (and life!), and I am so proud of you for sticking to it.

You have reached the place in this book where you may become distracted by other things—starting a new book, rearranging your bedroom, browsing Instagram—simply because I am welcoming you into taking everything we've talked about so far and <u>putting it into action</u>. That means you *doing the things*: some things that you haven't done before, some things that are uncomfortable, and some things that will bring up deep-rooted fears and doubts. I know you're going to become distracted because it happens to me too.

We tend to get really fired up while reading a self-empowerment book, visualizing all the ways we'll step into our power and shift our mindset, but when it comes to getting down and dirty with the actual commitments that create the change . . . well, we lose a bit of that fire. But not this time. This time you're not alone. This time you have a whole resource section of tools to begin practicing and implementing daily. This time you have me by your side, through these words and the magic of social media. So I want you to take a big deep breath and congratulate yourself for being so committed to YOU! As you know now, YOU are the common denominator of every experience in your life, so for all the time and energy you've already dedicated to YOU, those benefits and growth are already on their way!

I've read many self-help books that absolutely inspired me, but once I completed the book, that inspiration dwindled. I would have the concepts in my mind, but I never felt clear on *how* to take *action* to bring these concepts into MY LIFE. This lack of knowing always frustrated me, and I vowed that through my coaching, through my events, and when I wrote my first book, I would ensure that every person who received teachings from me *had access* to the tools required to make the changes they desired immediately.

And let's face it; that's why we're all here, right? We want to create *change and growth,* not just read about it. We want to experience undeniable *joy and happiness.* Well, the upcoming tools you're about to learn about and practice—they hold the power to create that change for you!

Now, can I be real for a second? You already *have* the knowledge, wisdom, and tools accessible to you. Most of these tools are not going to be brand new to you. Even if you've never practiced them, chances are you've heard of them, or your sister-in-law mentioned something similar, or you saw a YouTube video about them. You've likely even heard of these tools from another teacher before, or you have used something similar. That's perfect, because this book is designed to **reignite your awareness of the power you possess to heal yourself from within**.

These tools are like your personal handbook for mastering your emotions, your mind, your body, and your life. I want you to feel so confident, so empowered, and believe so strongly that you CAN heal any wounds, take on any projects, be completely and wholly happy, and live fulfilled from the inside out because you *know* that you *are* a perfect balance of the Divine Feminine and Divine Masculine!

Are you ready? Let's have some fun.

> These tools will help you remove the veils of lies that cover your consciousness and reveal the life that reflects the Truth of who you are—the Truth of your purpose here in this world.

And while they do this for you, here are some words of awareness as you dive in:

Sometimes when we become clear of that vision of our True Self, it can begin to feel a bit debilitating because our meaning-making machines (Ego brains) are so accustomed to finding proof of the contrary. We are so used to living with our suffering and doubt and victim mindset that even catching a glimpse of what is truly possible for us can make us squeamish and run for the hills—the hills being your old patterns of self-sabotage.

When we notice the distance between where we are now, and where we desire to be, our Ego mind likes to pipe up and remind us of the mistruths:

You've never stuck to a morning routine, so what makes you think you will now?

No one will support you with these changes; do you really want to be all alone forever?

Sure it works for them, but you're so needy it'll never work for you . . .

Anytime you notice a thought anywhere near ones like these, I want you to physically shake your head and say out loud, *NO!*

You have come too far to give up on yourself.

Let the essence and words of our soul mentor, Louise Hay, guide you: "You have been criticizing yourself for years and it hasn't worked. Try approving of yourself and see what happens." (*You Can Heal Your Life*)

Come back to that moment when you received this book. Maybe you bought it online, maybe you received it as gift. However these words came to you, come back to the energy of that moment now.

Why did you say yes? What about this book intrigued you? What hopes and dreams did you associate with this book?

I can say with complete confidence that if your soul wasn't guiding you to receive and embody something in these messages, you would not have picked up this book. It just wouldn't have happened. You would have known intuitively that *Feminine Warrior* is not for you, and if it still somehow made its way into your lap, you wouldn't have made it this far through.

You are here. With me. And all the other women who are reading these words at this exact moment! I am so incredibly grateful for that. Because with the way the world has been pumping out trauma and fear and hatred in 2020, we need YOU in your **strength** and **empowerment**, now more than ever!

You've made it to the final section, so can we both get real and have you agree to simply stay committed to the end and acknowledge that the untrue gremlin in your mind is exactly that—untrue? We all know your analytical and purpose-driven brain wants action items to make all the goodness on the previous pages become your reality. Don't worry; I promise to deliver. But I also want to remind you of what we learned in the Energetic Alignment section: *it's so much less about the action itself; it's ALL about the intention and energy behind that action!*

This section is not about you doing all the things, all the time. That's a recipe for overwhelm and burnout, which I have a feeling you're ready to leave behind you. Instead, I want you to intentionally and consciously choose which practices you are intuitively drawn to play with first. Trust that there is an energetic reason and intuitive guidance from your soul behind the subtle draw toward them. Hold the belief in your mind that you are receiving *exactly* what you need.

You are welcome to come back to this section at any time to revisit the practices you skimmed over. Let this section become your "go-to" resource for self-healing, personal development, morning practices, and your inner-empowerment journey.

Whether you are committing to a thirty-day fitness challenge, waking up at 5:30 a.m. on weekdays, or creating another income stream for your family, the only way you will stay committed to your goal is by being committed to your WHY! This commitment is absolutely essential if you desire to create any kind of sustainable change.

As you open yourself to your more feminine qualities and energy, you will start to feel life more fully. You will experience everything to a deeper degree. I call this experience *living a sensual life*. Your body's whispers become louder. Your intuition will become harder to ignore. You will be unable to turn a blind eye to the mistruths you once believed to simply be "the way the world works." It is both a blessing of your awakening and a disaster for your Ego.

In order for you to achieve goals in your new state of balanced masculine and feminine energy, your goal has to touch deeper into your being than the surface level desires you craved before.

It's no longer about just reaching that next income level to buy more things; it becomes about the new ways you can invest that money into yourself and others and how you will feel with that level of abundance and prosperity every day. It's no longer about wanting to lose weight to fit in your skinny jeans; it becomes about how differently you hold your body and interact with the world when you feel immense confidence from your higher level of self-care and love. It's no longer about trying to meditate because you know you should; it becomes about noticing the difference in your energetic vibration and ability to connect with your intuition from committing to a daily practice and ritual.

Getting clear on your deeper emotional and energetic WHY is how we create goals with soul. When we have goals that are aligned with our soul's desires, it becomes easy and graceful to move toward achieving them, and they are achieved in a sustainable and nourishing way.

It is about saying no to the societal conditioning that *being busy = being better* and *all success must come from hard work and sacrifice.*

When you are balanced in your masculine and feminine energies, you stop sacrificing your well-being to achieve an external goal and you begin aligning yourself internally with the energetic vibration and emotional qualities of that version of yourself who has already achieved that goal. When we are in that soul alignment, the action we take produces far greater results with significantly less effort.

Wait, did you actually take that sentence in? Let me repeat it for you.

When we are in that soul alignment, the action we take produces far greater results with significantly less effort.

This is the "Do Less, Be More" concept! And it's totally accessible to you, right now. You *do less and be more* through spiritual practice and daily devotions—to yourself, to your energy, to your Source/Universe/Spirit/God, to your craft and creativity.

But how, Deanna? you might be wondering, which is why I am going to share another personal story of embodying my own feminine warrior with you.

In late 2019 I had an amazing experience while testing out the whole quantum leaping concept for the first time. I had just hosted my first conference, which was incredible, but I was plagued by this feeling of insecurity, fear of lack, and worry about the future, and I thought that I wasn't *doing* enough to sustain any success in my life. It was this nagging feeling that I had just experienced a *one-time* success and that this trajectory would not continue.

I hated these feelings because to the public eye, I was killin' it. My online engagement had grown significantly, and it was very noticeable. I received daily messages from people celebrating my growth and impact, but I couldn't fully receive them because I couldn't *feel* it. I wouldn't let myself out of fear that all this success would all slip through my fingers soon. I just spiraled deeper and deeper into my own victim mindset—my mentality of lack, of fear, of worry and doubt.

I knew something had to change, and I was far along enough in my spiritual journey to know that anything I desire to change *out there* must first begin *in here*. So I sat with myself, in this uncomfortable emotion, and asked for guidance. *What am I supposed to do to change? How can I return to seeing through the eyes of love? What am I not doing that I need to do in order to be who I want to be and have what I want to have?*

The questions in my journal went on and on and on. And on. And on, for weeks! Then one day I had an epiphany. The ONLY thing I had yet to commit myself one hundred percent fully to was a daily devotional practice. Yet, I was hesitant about the concept of doing the same thing every single day. I hate the feeling of being addicted to or reliant on anything, even if it's a positive daily action. One of my core values has always been FREEDOM, and I prided myself on NOT committing to any one thing each day. I pushed and forced away any ideas of consistency that brought up these feelings. Well, it turns out daily devotional practice was the ONE thing I had yet to try with any solid commitment. And at that point in my life, the pain of the victim mindset was far stronger than the pain of trying something new.

And so I began my daily devotional practice. It looked like this:

Every morning when I first woke up, I dedicated AT LEAST thirty minutes to my spiritual practices.

- Ten minutes moving my body organically on my yoga mat: a combination of cat/cow, gentle child's pose, spinal swirls and twirls, and breath work.

- Ten minutes in quiet meditation either asking for guidance or simply being open to receiving whatever wisdom was there for me to receive.

- Ten minutes journaling on my reflections from both organic movement and meditation, thirty things of gratitude, and any other thoughts and desires that wanted to be expressed.

This was my commitment for a MINIMUM of thirty days. I began a new journal (one that was oh-so-beautiful), and some days I would write one page, some days I would write five. This time was dedicated just to me, just to my own learning and growing and expanding. In time I added reading to my morning routine, at least a few pages (or chapters depending on the day) from an author I admired and was excited to learn from.

And now, as I write these words, my daily devotional practice is anywhere from forty-five minutes to two hours and includes a kundalini kriya, EFT Tapping with affirmations, and chanting a few mantras. This time is my own educational growth and spiritual

surrender. I don't attend any form of church, so I use this time as
my time at church, surrendering my own needs and desires and
showing up in service to love.

When I first began this daily devotional practice, I made it a priority to seek new knowledge, new perspectives, and new tools for MYSELF. This was huge. For five years prior, every training or course I took was for MY CLIENTS. I gained knowledge for the sole purpose of then sharing it and teaching it to my clients. But this time was about ME. And yes, in time I would inevitably share it with my clients—it'd be rude not to—but the *intention* was different. It was about me, my journey, my growth, and my openness to devote myself to the higher powers, the teachers, the wisdom around me.

There were mornings, of course, when I absolutely didn't want to do it. Instead of not doing it, I journaled on my resistance. I became more aware of my desperate need to be *doing* and feel *productive* and explored why that was so important to me. And there were times when I received crystal clear guidance from my meditation, and sometimes I spent the entire time trying to redirect my thoughts away from the many future and past scenarios that were playing out in my mind. It was a far-from-*perfect* experience each day, and for that I am grateful.

What happened in time was that it became my natural state. I felt off if I went a morning without it (especially weekends). I came to crave it, to love it. I started waking up at 5:00 a.m., an entire one-and-a-half hours earlier than I normally did, just to have more time to spend in this devotional practice. I prayed to the Universe, and

I gave thanks and gratitude for my breath, my body, my mind, my home, my life, my Dixie, my everything. I gave thanks for the entire world, for the women and men and babies and animals. I came so deep into a state of complete surrender and gratitude about everything that my life became an unfolding of magic.

I had to be DILIGENT with my thoughts around money, lack, and fear during this process. Each time I noticed my thoughts drift toward *"How am I going to pay for that?"* or *"I sure hope someone wants some coaching soon,"* I made a clear and conscious choice to pray for guidance and ask that the Universe redirect my thoughts. I asked to see through the eyes of love. I asked to see the beauty and abundance and joy of my life. I asked to see things differently, to feel the love instead of the lack. It wasn't easy, but it did feel good when I could create that shift.

And then, right about the time that I noticed I had almost completely filled my new journal, exactly thirty days after I began, I felt it. I felt the shift. The quantum leap. Within one week I had so many amazing synchronicities occur:

- I was offered a keynote speaking role at an amazing women in business leadership conference.

- A woman, whom I love, chose to register for my New Zealand retreat.

- A local client who had joined some of my in-person workshops and online programs reached out to explore coaching and ended up signing up for six months of 1:1 coaching.

- Another woman who had just begun showing up for my weekly Friday morning show on Facebook asked about coaching and ended up saying yes to joining my six-month Mastery program.

- I received incredible testimonials from previous clients almost every day about how amazing my coaching is and how much it changed their lives.

The clients I was serving at the time were having incredible results and experiences within their lives.

My interaction and engagement online went up tenfold. It was super fun to show up online with so many engaged and interested women!

In those seven days, I secured over $10,000 for my company, which was the *exact amount* I needed to reach my 2019 income goal that had eluded me for months and months. I had spent the majority of 2019 asking myself, *"How am I going to achieve this goal? How have I not got there yet . . . why is this so hard for me? Maybe I'm not meant to earn money doing what I love."*

All the fears and worries and doubts rolled in all year long. And then, when I least expected it, when I focused on devotion and giving and gratitude INSTEAD of the "how to get" mentality, I reached my goal. *I achieved what I desired. It happened, and it was easy.*

This is the power of feminine flow, of authentic surrender, of co-creating with the Universe. This is the ability that every single one of us has within us when we stop trying to control and dictate and contort our lives to follow the exact outline we've created in our minds. **Remember, we don't know what we don't know.**

So don't allow your limited thinking to dictate what is possible for you. Let yourself dream. Let yourself feel what is possible, because if you can envision it in your mind, if you can feel it in your body, even if it feels completely unattainable, it can become your reality. Sink deeply into your *why*, your raison d'être, your reason for being. That'll power you up and keep you going, even on days where you feel like you don't have it in you.

Just before we get into the actual embodiment practices, I want to share with you my two-fold WHY for creating this book:

One, I am already offering so much in the way of content and teachings and resources to my community online that it simply feels like the perfect next step to compile it all in a book that is tangible, re-readable, and easy to digest. But that reason isn't what keeps me up at night, writing new chapters at 1:00 a.m. or rereading it over and over to ensure it delivers the most powerful experience possible. Nope, that's just a pleasant by-product of the work.

The real, deep-rooted, core *why* is that I am not willing to die with this music still inside me. I have known since I was a young girl that my words have healing power—I didn't know what that meant, or how it would ever be used, but from my childhood I could see myself on stage, sharing my words, and witnessing the audience being uplifted and elevated because of it. This image has been a constant in my life, especially in my darkest days. I see myself as someone capable and able to help another heal. I have seen it over the years when friends and colleagues have turned to me for advice or support or love. I am honored to play this role.

When I was nineteen, I lost my mom to cancer. It was devastating and heartbreaking. And I didn't get a chance to share my truths with her—to share my view of the world with her in a way that could inspire and uplift her. As is common with her baby-boomer generation, my mom was an expert at keeping her emotions hidden underneath her pleasantries. When we went shopping, for example, it didn't matter if she needed anything for herself, she would always focus her attention on me and my sister, putting whatever we needed above her own needs. Her sanctuary was to cuddle on the couch in the living room, reading her book, and drifting off to a faraway land. If my mom were here today, she could hear my words, she could receive the healing gifts I have, and perhaps, just perhaps, her body would still be healthy and well!

The knowledge that there are MILLIONS of women in this world who feel their emotions are not valid, who are suppressing their feelings daily to "fit in" with society, and who compare themselves to others to the point of self-depreciation gets under my skin and makes me so hot with rage that I could burst. And if there is anything that I can say, do, express, or be that will create change for even one of those women, I am completely, whole-heartedly, ridiculously committed to doing it.

So when I am tired, don't want to write, and feel uninspired, I do two things:

1. I honor my feelings and ask my intuition what I truly need, and
2. Then I do that thing.

Honestly, it works every time. I don't have to force myself into this goal because it is already so deeply engrained in my cells. I do create structure and discipline around my writing, however, such as creating space every day to write if I feel inspired and ensuring my body is nourished with daily movement and healthy food—these are must-haves to keep my energy flowing.

Writing out intimate details of my life and displaying my beliefs and teachings on paper for the world to see are obviously not exactly *easy* things to do. But can you see that my *why* is so strong that it trumps the fear and the worry and the doubt and the emotion? It allows me to stay committed, in my heart, to the bigger picture. And with that soulful alignment, the inspired action always presents itself. So as we journey through this section together and you focus on the change you want to create, in yourself and the world, please keep the following questions in mind:

- *What is your deeper why?*

- *What is the burning desire within your heart that will allow you to show up and commit, even on the hard days, even on the sad days, even when no one else can see that vision with you?*

I am taking a stand that we women, that all human beings, no longer need to suffer from our social conditioning, attachment to external validation, and obsession with fear. I am taking a stand for an end to racism, oppression, hate-fueled destruction, unnecessary hunger, unsupported mental health, cruelty to animals, burning of forests, and polluting the ocean. The vision that I hold dear to my heart is the day that we ALL take soulful responsibility for our own actions and beliefs, when we understand the innate power and strength we have within ourselves to heal and awaken, and when we are able to put others first because we are already WHOLE and overflowing with love.

That is the world I want to live in.

That is the world where we share our resources with our neighbors near and far.

That is the world where we offer a smile to strangers in small towns and big cities, where we spend thousands of dollars on feeding people rather than attending a concert or sports game, and where every single one of us feels safe to be ourselves.

Begin your journey home to the feminine warrior you already are, with a little help from your intuitive life coach, Dea.

I have categorized each of these embodiment resources into sections. These sections are part of my Signature Teaching; *The Four Pillars of Personal Mastery*:

Physical Well-Being
Emotional Resiliency
Mental Clarity
Spiritual Awakenings

Our lives are infused with the teachings of each one, overlapping in the most beautiful and intricate ways. Earlier in the book we learned that we are nothing more than energy, so therefore, as holistic beings, when we take action in one area in our life, all other areas are affected. While I've categorized each technique in one of the four pillars, remember that any action that affects one area of your being will also affect all others. So know that when you are focused on physical well-being, you are also reaping spiritual benefits as well. And when you are building that emotional resiliency, you are also gaining mental clarity too. Honor the holistic influence of you as a whole, a beautiful, bountiful, empowered whole.

PHYSICAL WELL-BEING

MIRROR GAZING

WHAT AND WHY

Have you ever noticed how much babies and children love looking at themselves in the mirror? They have this beautiful love affair with their own reflection, talking to themselves, and observing how their bodies move when they speak. It's quite entertaining to watch. When they look in the mirror, they see their magnificence. That's why it's so addicting to keep looking. They are not looking at their flaws or their bulges or their wrinkles or their insecurities. They are seeing their brilliance and their magnitude of beauty and perfection. It is this kind of radical self-love that we adults need as well, but many of us are too uncomfortable to even look into our own eyes for more than a few seconds to put on mascara. This mirror technique is about connecting with your essence—your soul. It goes beyond your physical appearance. It's about becoming comfortable with who you are and seeing the magnificence of your being. We all have it, we are all magnificent, it's just a matter of whether you allow yourself to see it within you. When you practice this technique regularly, you will notice a deep, calm presence of self-acceptance emerge. Others will notice it too. It is you saying *YES* to yourself—it is you honoring your gifts, your beauty, your wisdom, and your essence. It is going beyond the layers of self-doubt and your inner critic and choosing to see the depth of your soul. It truly is powerful healing wrapped up in a very simplistic practice.

WHEN TO USE THIS TECHNIQUE

The more challenging this technique is for you to do at the beginning dictates how often you should do it. If it is very uncomfortable and challenging, aim to use this practice every day. As you become more accustomed to it, you can soften the number of times you commit to. I recommend you practice mirror gazing no less than once or twice a week.

THE PRACTICE

Begin by sitting in a comfortable position in front of your mirror. You may be sitting cross-legged on a pillow or resting against your bed or couch nearby. You'll want to be fairly close to the mirror, so you can truly gaze directly into your own eyes.

Once you are physically comfortable, close your eyes and say a gentle prayer or set an intention that your mirror gazing will be an experience of true authentic love and peace. Take a few deep breaths through your nose and exhale through your mouth. This breath work helps to calm any nerves and connect you more deeply with the present moment.

As you open your eyes, look through the mirror into your own eyes and hold your gaze. It may feel uncomfortable or silly or weird, and that's okay. Hold your own gaze so intently that your external peripheral vision begins to blur and all you can see is you. It's very common to be overcome with emotion here, so allow the tears to blur your eyes and flow down your cheeks. You are truly seeing yourself for the first time. You are connecting with your essence, your soul, in a completely nonjudgmental and intimate way. You are observing your own magnificence.

Hold your gaze for as long as you can. Aim for at least one to two minutes the first few times, then gradually extend to five to ten minutes.

You may receive intuitive guidance in the form of visions, sensations, thoughts, and feelings. Allow these to be present. You may want to give up and stop your eye gazing, but use your inner resiliency in this process and trust yourself to continue recommitting to you.

ENERGY HEALING—SELF-PRACTICE

WHAT AND WHY

We are energetic beings made up of specific energy compilations that create our physical reality, including our homes, our cars, and our bodies. As with all of nature, we have the inherent gift of healing within our own bodies. Our skin knows to scab when we are cut, our body knows to vomit when we've eaten something poisonous or rotten, and we have cravings for specifics foods and drink when we are out of balance. The same is true for our ability to heal through intentional energy work on ourselves. When we use the powerful combination of cognitive intention with physical embodiment, we create an environment of deep energy healing. We create an environment that promotes our energy to come back into balance. Whenever we have physical or emotional pain, we are out of alignment and balance. The purpose of energy work is to come back to balance, just like nature is always in dynamic movement finding its way back to homeostasis.

The more you use this practice, the more you will be able to feel and notice the results of it. The healing is occurring whether you can see it or not, but as human beings, we do love to see physical results, so keep using this practice so you notice the results.

WHEN TO USE THIS TECHNIQUE

You are welcome to repeat these sessions as many times as desired, sometimes multiple times a day depending on your needs. You will find that you'll turn to this practice when you feel physical pain, but I encourage you to use it even when no pain or discomfort is present. This technique can be a proactive tool to help you stay in energetic alignment and flow.

THE PRACTICE

When you begin using this practice, it is best to bring yourself to a sacred space of healing. This space may be a specific room in your house, it may be near an altar you've created with inspirational messages and candles and crystals, or it may be outside in the summer with your toes in the grass. Choose a sacred space that is healing and nourishing for you, where you feel safe. Commit to doing your energy healing in this space for at the least the first few times as it will help your nervous system and mind to relax into the experience by being in a familiar environment.

Energy healing occurs at all times, but in order for you to become more intentional and present with your experience, it's best to come into a meditative state to release your attachment to thoughts. You are welcome to use any of the meditations in this book or simply use your breath to come into your body and the present moment.

Once you feel present, begin vigorously rubbing your hands together to generate heat between your palms. Your palms are the center point for the energy to flow. Begin asking your hands to guide you to where healing energy is needed. You may immediately feel a gentle pull toward a specific spot in your body, or you may sit in silence and deep breath for a few moments until guidance occurs. Both are perfect.

When your hands find their way to a place on your body, allow them to rest on your skin or just above it in your energetic field. As your hands rest there, envision the most beautiful and healing golden light flowing from the palms of your hands to this place in your body. Envision any pain or discomfort as a specific color, then begin seeing that color gently melt away as the golden light replaces it. Allow your hands to rest in that spot until you feel guided to move somewhere else. Your hands may move to another spot on your body, in which case you will repeat the previous steps, or you may feel complete with the healing session and you can say a gentle prayer of gratitude and love to close your energy session.

BREATH WORK

WHAT AND WHY

Breath work, or pranayama in yogic philosophy, is the process of changing your unconscious breathing patterns and making them intentional and conscious. This breathing helps the body and mind balance and alleviates stress caused by overstimulation of the nervous system. Our common tendency is to breathe shallow quick breaths all day long, never allowing the lungs to expand to their full capacity or the brain to be fully oxygenated. Breathing this way activates the sympathetic nervous system which is our "fight or flight" response and causes undue stress on the body. When we slow down and create intentional breathing patterns, we activate the parasympathetic nervous system, which naturally reduces stress, anxiety, and worry.

In ancient yogic philosophy we are made up of five different bodies or layers of energy called the Koshas. When you are using intentional breathing techniques, you are working in your Breath Body—the pranayama kosha.

Pranayama breathing techniques are consciously working in our Breath Body to create balance, alleviate stress, and cultivate a sense of overall harmony in body and mind. There are many ways you can breathe consciously, and each way allows a different part of your subtle bodies to awaken and produce healing experiences. The following is a list of three of the most common breath work techniques that I have learned and use often.

3-PART BELLY BREATH

WHEN TO USE THIS TECHNIQUE

The 3-part Belly Breath technique is very useful when you are feeling overwhelmed, anxious, or worried. It calms the mind and soothes the muscles. It is a powerful support for stress, insomnia, and physical tension.

THE PRACTICE

Begin in a comfortable seated position with your spine long and tall, or lying flat on your back. Place one hand on your chest and one on your belly. Close your eyes and bring your awareness inside your body and away from your thoughts. Notice your natural breath, the length of the inhale and exhale, and set an intention for your pranayama practice.

Begin your 3-part breath. Slowly inhale fully until you notice your chest rise, then your upper abdomen rise, then your belly puff out like a balloon. Slowly release your breath first from your belly, then your abdomen, then your chest. Repeat this cycle for as long as feels good in your body, usually five to ten rounds.

When you return to your natural breath, stay centered with your eyes closed and notice how your body feels after this practice. Has your body softened any tension? Have you released your attachment to that thought you previously couldn't shake? Do you feel peaceful and calm?

If you'd like to deepen your practice, allow yourself to slip into a meditation from this place.

ALTERNATE NOSTRIL BREATHING—IN SANSKRIT, IT'S KNOWN AS NADI SHODHANA PRANAYAMA

WHEN TO USE THIS TECHNIQUE
This practice is powerful when you are too "in your head" about something. When we are overly cognitive, this breath technique brings our right and left brain hemispheres into balance.

THE PRACTICE
This breath technique is designed to clear and purify your prana channels and balance your right and left brain activity. It is also a useful tool in balancing masculine and feminine energy.

Begin in a comfortable seated position, with your spine long and tall. Close your eyes and bring your awareness inside your body and away from your thoughts. Notice your natural breath, the length of the inhale and exhale, and set an intention for your pranayama practice.

Using your right hand, place your thumb gently on your right nostril and your ring finger gently on your left nostril. Your middle and pointer finger may reach up to your third eye—the center of your forehead—while your pinky finger rests comfortably on your face. Begin alternate nostril breathing. Using your thumb, gently press into your nostril to stop the flow of breath as you inhale fully through your left nostril only. Inhale for a count of five. Use your ring finger to close your left nostril (now both nostrils are restricted) and hold for a count of five. Release your right thumb and exhale slowly through your right nostril for a count of five. Close both nostrils and hold your lungs empty for a count of five.

Repeat this cycle for as long as feels good in your body, usually five to ten rounds. Focus your mind on following the pathway of your breath, in one nasal channel and out the other. This breathing aids in the balancing of both masculine and feminine energy.

When you return to your natural breath, stay centered with your eyes closed and notice how your body feels after this practice. Do you feel more balanced between your nasal channels? What part of your body feels activated and alive? What part of your body feels settled and calm?

If you'd like to deepen your practice, allow yourself to slip into a meditation from this place.

BREATH OF FIRE—IN SANSKRIT: KAPALABAHTI

WHEN TO USE THIS TECHNIQUE
This technique is a great tool to use right before a yoga practice or workout to invigorate the body before your physical movement. It

is also useful when feeling anxious or depressed to bring you back to a neutral inner alignment.

THE PRACTICE

This powerful and invigorating breath technique helps cleanse your entire being and builds inner core strength. Using this technique regularly helps cleanse the lungs and diaphragm, detox the body by increasing blood circulation, and oxygenate the brain for heightened mental stimulation. You may feel slightly light-headed, which is completely normal, but please listen to your body. Having a box of tissues nearby is handy as it's quite a cleansing pranayama.

Note: This practice should be avoided if you are pregnant, menstruating, or have high blood pressure.

Begin in a comfortable seated position, with your spine long and tall. Close your eyes and bring your awareness inside your body and away from your thoughts. Notice your natural breath, the length of the inhale and exhale, and set an intention for your pranayama practice.

Place one hand on your abdomen and begin to breathe in and out of your nose. With each exhale, pull your abdomen in toward your spine and then gently expand your abdomen out with each inhale. Begin to find a rhythm where both inhale and exhale are equal in length, then start to quicken your pace. Your breath should be loud and quick, similar to the sound of dog panting. Continue this quick breathing for approximately thirty seconds. When you pause, take intentionally long and calming breaths and focus your attention on how your body feels. After a few calming breaths, begin again. Aim for two to three rounds of thirty seconds each with long nourishing breaths in between rounds.

When you return to your natural breath, stay centered with your eyes closed and notice how your body feels after this practice. Can you feel your subtle energy body invigorated and alive? What do you notice in your abdomen after such intense movement and breath?

ENERGY-RELEASE TECHNIQUE

WHAT AND WHY

Every thought and emotion that we have consists of molecules of energy in our body. When we hold those thoughts or emotions inside ourselves, it creates a buildup of energy that needs to be released. When it isn't intentionally released, it often explodes out of you in inopportune times like in a social setting, or yelling at your kids, or saying things you don't mean to your partner. Using this Energy-Release technique allows all stagnant energy to be released from your body in a sacred and healthy way, creating more spaciousness and neutrality in your body.

WHEN TO USE IT THIS TECHNIQUE

This tool is a powerful one to use in the moment of heightened emotion. It can also be used to assist in alleviating physical pain and releasing any energy you've embodied from others. I personally have gone from agonizing pain in my body to complete peace and calm simply from doing this practice. You'll also notice that children and animals, especially dogs, use this technique regularly to "shake off" energy and transition to a neutral state.

THE PRACTICE

Begin by creating a sacred space where you can be as loud as possible and your body is free from hitting objects around you. You are going to have an intentional version of a temper tantrum with the focus of releasing energy from your body.

Start in a standing position and shake your hands and wrists while rising up and down on your heels. Let the energy and momentum build within you as you speed up your movement. Allow your arms and legs and head to flail erratically, shaking, twisting, and pounding your whole body into the air. Allow yourself to fully surrender into the process. You may fall to the ground and pound your fists into the carpet/earth. You may jump up and down as you pound your feet into the ground. You may shake your whole body so intensely that you lose your footing and stumble to the ground. Let your WHOLE body be released. Shake it out completely until you feel exhausted and a sense of energetic emptiness.

Once you feel ready to calm your energy, lie or sit on the floor and place one hand on your heart and one hand on your belly. Breathe in deeply, close your eyes, and hold yourself with the deepest love you can imagine. It may help to envision yourself as your eight-year-old self, scared, lost, and alone. Whisper sweet nothings to yourself as you hold your body. *Sweet nothings are when you take everything you wish anyone would say to you and you say them to yourself: "I*

love you. I appreciate you. I see you. I value you. You're beautiful.
It's okay. I've got you. I believe in you."

Allow yourself to stay in this position for as long as it takes until
you feel ready to transition out. Sometimes it will be a few moments,
sometimes a half hour or longer. I've had some releases when I cuddle
up to Dixie and fall asleep with tear-streaked cheeks. Allow yourself
the space and time to be fully present with your emotions and needs.
Be sure to drink plenty of water after your energy release and be
gentle with yourself, emotionally and physically. You've moved a lot
of energy and stirred up emotions, so take extra space to simply *be*.

EMOTIONAL RESILIENCY

EMOTIONAL TRIGGER RELEASE TECHNIQUE

WHAT AND WHY

The Emotional Trigger Release technique is a powerful tool to help you see your triggers as guideposts to creating new conscious habits and choices in your life. It allows you to take the frustration and annoyance of a triggered moment and transmute it into an opportunity to rewire your belief systems. Each time you move through all steps of this technique, you are creating new neural pathways into your consciously chosen beliefs. This tool brings your power back to you, helping you become crystal clear on what subconscious beliefs are playing behind the scenes of your mind that are no longer serving you. No more societal conditioning for you!

WHEN TO USE THIS TECHNIQUE

Every time you are triggered by something—what someone said at work, the house not being clean, your friend forgetting your birthday, the annoying woman at the grocery store. In the beginning you may want to use this technique in the safety and sacred space of your own home to allow time and space for your emotions to arise. In time, as you continue practicing, you'll be able to use this technique with a few deep breaths even when surrounded by people and triggers.

THE PRACTICE
There are six steps to this process. The more often you use them, the easier they will be to flow through with ease and minimal thought. The first few/many times you use them, I recommend you use your journal and flow slowly through each step.

STEP 1 ~ *TRIGGER*
Identify that something/someone has triggered an undesired emotion or thought in you. This is the *thing* that has happened.

STEP 2 ~ *EMOTION*
Identify what your primary emotion is—how you feel in relation to that thing happening.

STEP 3 ~ *FEAR/LIMITING BELIEF*
Identify what the deep-rooted fear or limiting belief is underneath this primary emotion. It may seem irrational or make no logical sense. That's okay!

Take a few breaths and let yourself feel into this fear/belief and identify there is no Truth to it. It is not your Truth, it is only a limiting belief. Breathe deeply. Be gentle with yourself. Place your hands on your body. Honor that little girl inside of you who fears this belief is true, and gently remind her it is not true! It is not your Truth.

STEP 4 ~ *SWEET NOTHINGS*

As you rest in this moment of awareness and acceptance of your discovered belief, begin to say everything you wish someone would say to you in this vulnerable moment:

"I love you; it's okay; this is just an irrational fear; it is not true; you are worthy of love; you are beautiful; you are loved; you are so precious and so important; you are amazing . . ."

Give yourself everything you want or need by whispering the sweet loving mantras and true statements to yourself. Hold your body with love and kindness. Energetically hold your heart with much care and grace. Be your own mama in this moment. Hold zero judgment, only pure acceptance, pure love, and pure belief in your True Self.

STEP 5 ~ *NEW BELIEF*

Explore:

- What do you choose to replace this fear/belief with?
- How do you desire to feel?
- What would you like your belief to be?
- What do you desire to believe?
- We have this power within us, the power to rewrite our belief systems. Don't underestimate how incredible you are. Choose a belief that feels EMPOWERING! A belief that feels incredible to write, to speak, to feel in your body.

STEP 6 ~ *EVIDENCE/PROOF*

Start seeking evidence and proof that this new belief is already true in all areas of your life. Begin by writing down all pieces of evidence you can think of right away and then revisit this new belief each morning in your journaling and record the many ways this belief is already manifesting in your life. Journaling is a crucial aspect of embodying this new belief. Without this step, your Ego will arise with evidence and proof of how your past fear/belief is more true . . . it is how our brain works. In this step you are taking your power back from your Ego and choosing, over and over and over again, to embody your new conscious belief.

EFT TAPPING

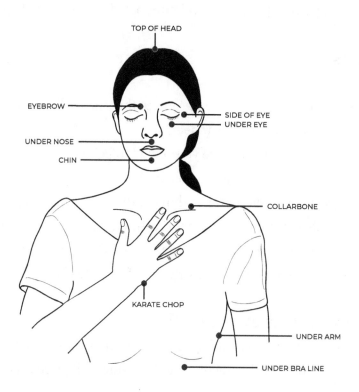

WHAT AND WHY

Emotional Freedom Technique is based on the ancient principles of Chinese medicine that we have energy channels flowing through our bodies. When these channels are flowing, we are in a natural state of health and wellness and happiness and well-being. When these channels become energetically blocked, the blockage leads to feelings of fear, worry, anxiety, doubt, disbelief, insecurity, judgment, and Ego mind. EFT Tapping guides you to physically tap on specific points on your body to activate your energy channels as you voice what it is that's causing some discomfort, harm, or fear.

This technique is designed to shine light on the negative emotions we feel so we can tap on our energetic meridians to free up the energy and alleviate the emotions. While practicing this technique, allow yourself to feel the emotions deep within your body. Do not be afraid to become emotional as you speak the negative feelings out loud. The more you can feel while tapping, the deeper into your subconscious this healing work will go.

"The fuel for effective tapping is voicing words that connect to the negative emotions, limiting beliefs and intensity of resistance you might feel when thinking about something you want to change."

~Margaret M. Lynch, Tapping into Wealth

I have been using EFT Tapping personally and with clients for years. The ability to lessen the intensity of any negative emotion within a few minutes is incredible. The key is to allow yourself to fully surrender to the process and not get hung up on the words you are saying or whether you are doing it right. If you can feel the negative energy, then you are doing it right!

WHEN TO USE THIS TECHNIQUE

Use this technique daily as a proactive emotional resiliency technique or whenever you feel emotionally unsettled. When you notice that you are wrapped up in a loop of Ego thought or negative emotion, use your EFT Tapping tool.

THE PRACTICE

Start by identifying the primary negative belief or emotion that you feel. For example, "I feel overwhelmed with stress." Tap three times on the side of the palm while activating your body's healing potential and preparing your mind and emotions for your tapping experience. "Even though I feel overwhelmed with stress, I still love and accept myself." Repeat this statement three times.

Then follow the visual tapping prompts while flowing through your emotional statements, getting deep into how you truly feel the deeper fears underneath those feelings. I've included a sample script you can follow for the primary belief of "I feel overwhelmed with stress."

Please see the link in the Additional Resources section for a video tutorial of this technique.

SAMPLE SCRIPT

Begin by tapping on the Karate Chop—side of one hand as seen in the illustration—and repeat this statement out loud three times: "Even though I feel this overwhelming stress, I am choosing to love and accept myself."

Flow through each tapping point with a statement.

EXAMPLE:

Tapping on the top of head: This stress is overwhelming.

Tapping on the top of eyebrow: I can't stand this feeling of stress.

Tapping on the side of eye: I want this stress to go away.

Tapping under the eye: This stress is wreaking havoc on my body.

Tapping under the nose: This stress is causing me so much pain.

Tapping on the chin: I shouldn't have this stress; I don't need this stress.

Tapping on the collarbone: I want this stress to go away; I don't like it.

Tapping under the arm: I am tired and done with all of this stress.

Tapping under the bra line: I hate this stress.

Tapping wrists together: If I could let this stress go away, I could finally be happy.

Return to top of head and continue to cycle through each tapping point in order while stating the following:

I'm ready for this stress to go away.

This stress is debilitating my ability to love.

This stress makes me feel like I am an inadequate person.

I feel stupid because of this stress; I feel stupid, stupid, stupid.

It makes me feel as if I am not good enough as who I am.

If only I could find a way to be good enough exactly as I am.

But that's never going to happen for me, is it?

That's what this stress does—makes me feel stupid.

I hate it; I hate this.

I want this stress to go away; I no longer need it.

Pause and take a few deep breaths. Notice how you feel in your body and mind. Ask yourself if you're ready to explore what it would feel like to no longer live with this stress. When you feel ready, begin again at the Karate Chop point and repeat this three times: "Even though I still have this stress, I am choosing to love and accept myself."

Continue through the tapping points with each statement, starting at the top of the head.

I'm better than this stress.

This stress doesn't own me.

I'm in charge here,

not this feeling of stress.

That's all it is, a feeling.

And feelings can change.

What would it be like if I didn't have this stressful feeling?

What would it feel like to release this stress?

I think I'm ready to release this stress.

This stress doesn't own me anymore.

I'm ready to let go of this stress.

I think I can do it; I think I can let go.

This is it; I'm ready.

Stress, I let you go.

Finally, I release you.

That's it. We're done.

Stress, I don't need you.

Stress, I'm okay without you.

This is my moment—to live stress-free.

Really, I believe it, I feel it, and I know it.

Stress, I let you go!

Pause and take a few deep breaths. Notice how you feel in your body and mind. Ask yourself if you're really ready to let all stress go. Ask what you would love to replace that stress with. When you feel ready, begin again at the Karate Chop point and repeat this three times: "Even though I allowed myself to feel stressed, I am choosing to love and accept myself."

Continue through the tapping points with each statement, starting at the top of the head.

I am ready to come into my own.

This moment now, is when I'm ready.

I believe in me.

I feel completely free and expansive.

Every time I breathe, I feel freer.

This feeling of freedom is incredible.

I've never felt such joy in my life.

Every cell in my being feels this sense of freedom.

I am full of freedom and love and calmness.

I can handle anything and everything that happens.

I trust myself.

I trust my choices.

I trust my actions.

I trust myself to handle every situation.

This is it; this is my moment.

I absolutely love and accept myself.

Pause, take a few deep inhales and exhales, close eyes and simply sit with this new belief. If you feel inspired, open your journal and write out your experience and how you feel now.

CONSCIOUS COMMUNICATION

WHAT AND WHY

As human beings, one of our primary needs is to feel that we belong. We deeply desire to be a part of a group, collective, or community in some way, which means that a primary function of our being is to engage in relationships with others. Whether these relationships are with your partner or close family, colleagues and coworkers, social network, clients or strangers, there are powerful techniques we can use to ensure our communication with others is conscious and clear. These techniques allow for others to feel seen, acknowledged, and heard when they engage with us, allowing our relationship with them to be of service to their (and our) highest good. When human beings practice conscious communication, there are fewer unnecessary arguments, long-standing resentments, triggering conversations, feelings of isolation, and hatred between people.

While you never have control over how someone else will respond to you, you always have the power (and responsibility) of consciously communicating from your heart. These tools will support you in being a good listener and holder of space for others in your life.

WHEN TO USE THIS TECHNIQUE
Every. Single. Day.

THE PRACTICE
When engaging with another person, these are a few simple things you can do to ensure the other person feels seen and acknowledged and that you are communicating effectively.

Body Language ~ Allow your body to visually represent your interest in the other person. Allow your shoulders to face the person you're listening to, keep your hands relaxed and calm, and keep your gaze at the other person's eyes. Many people find direct eye contact very intimidating, but don't let this phase you. We all desire to be deeply and truly seen by another, especially someone with whom we feel safe. Hold their gaze with an open heart and mind.

Eliminate Distractions ~ Put your phone away, turn down the TV volume (or off all together), pause what you're doing so you can be fully present with them, even if it's only for one minute.

Ask Questions ~ Resist the urge to solve their problem by offering solutions; instead, ask open-ended questions to support them in finding their own solution.

Hold Space ~ This technique is less of an action and more of an intention. By consciously doing the actions above and making a choice to be present with this person, you are energetically holding space for their experience. Whether they are sharing a funny story, seeking a solution to a problem, or just talking about their day, having the intention to hold space for them is a powerful way to help them feel safe, seen, and loved in the conversation.

WRITE A LETTER TO YOUR INNER CHILD

WHAT AND WHY

Our childhood moments create recurring patterns and beliefs that play out regularly in our adult life. As you dive more deeply into your healing and spiritual awakening, you are likely to uncover moments from your past that feel painful, hurtful, and sad. This practice is a powerful tool to reconnect with your little girl inside, to offer her love and compassion, and to move toward deep energetic healing both in the past and the present.

WHEN TO USE THIS TECHNIQUE

Writing a letter to your younger self is such a powerful tool when you feel emotions arise that stem from a core moment of trauma or fear that occurred at a younger age. Your inner child still carries this pain, and it is likely manifesting in your present reality in unfavorable ways. This letter is a journey toward healing that past wound and allowing your little inner girl to feel safe, loved, protected, and expansive.

THE PRACTICE

Choose the age of yourself that you are writing to and spend a few moments feeling into her. What was her top priority at this time in life? What did she feel daily? What was she most concerned about? How safe or not did she feel with herself and with others? Once you feel connected to her, begin writing a letter of love and acceptance for who she is. Let her know that you forgive her for any choices she made, that she is loved and valued exactly as she is, and that she does not need to prove herself in any way. Write to her about how proud you are of her, how important she is, and how you are so grateful for her presence. Write everything to this younger version of you that you wish you had heard at the time. Tell her everything she needs and wants to hear, and allow it to flow from your heart. Let your tears stain the paper as you write all the wonderful ways that she brings love and light to this world. Let her know that none of it is her fault, that you believe her and believe in her, and always will. Let her feel safe. And when your letter feels complete, take a few moments to just sit with this energy transmission. How does it feel to share those words and energy with your younger self? Did any new insights arise? How are you feeling in the now-present moment? When you are complete, you may save the letter to read again one day or bless those words and offer it to the Universe in a ceremonial burning, maybe by candle flame or a campfire outside.

MENTAL CLARITY

FUTURE CASTING

WHAT AND WHY

One of the most powerful tools we possess is visualization. When used to its fullest potential, it engages both the mind and body to believe that what you are visualizing is occurring in the present moment. We use this tool every day but often not with conscious awareness; therefore, we end up creating a reality that reflects our thoughts, which often equates to our fears. This exercise will help you consciously awaken your soul's desires and invite them into your physical reality by visualizing them to be true right now. Allow yourself to truly feel the vision in your body. The more you can create a physical sensation, the faster you will manifest this reality for yourself!

WHEN TO USE THIS TECHNIQUE

Use this practice weekly or anytime you feel called to. Keep all your Future Casts in a safe place so you can look back when your dreams start to manifest for you! Have fun dreaming up your incredible future, and remember—the more you can feel this visualization to be true right now, the more likely it is to become true.

THE PRACTICE

The prompts below are your starting point. I suggest you set a timer for five to ten minutes, start with these statements, then record your visualization in your journal. Begin by choosing a set day and location in the future. You may choose one month from now, or ten years from now; there are no limits to your ability to manifest your future. Record how you are feeling on this particular day and location and begin completing the rest of the statements from this version of you.

For a printable Future Casting worksheet, please visit the link in Additional Resources at the end of the book.

Date: _____

Location: _____

I feel: _____

I am so grateful for: _____

I have accomplished/created: _____

I am finally proud of myself because: _____

The most incredible part of my life right now is: _____

_____

For me to create this life it truly took: _____

I've never been happier because: _____

GRATITUDE PRACTICE—DEANNA STYLE

WHAT AND WHY

A gratitude practice is like a daily guide to embody an attitude of gratitude and create a foundation for soulful manifestation. Gratitude is the fastest way to transform your world on the outside. It creates an internal world of appreciation and joy that aligns you energetically with receiving even more of what you love. It also helps to shift negative thought patterns into appreciation and abundance that support both emotional resiliency and mental clarity! Commit to this practice every single day and watch your life transform before your eyes.

WHEN TO USE THIS TECHNIQUE

You can use this technique as part of your daily morning practice or as a monthly reset during a new or full moon ceremony. Check out the Additional Resources section for a printable version of this technique.

THE PRACTICE

Take a piece of paper and draw a line down the center to create two columns. Label the column on the left "Current Amazingness" and the column on the right "Future Desires."

Current Amazingness is the column to record everything you are grateful for in this moment—physical things, experiences you've had, people, animals, everything that has been manifested already.

Future Desires is the column to record everything you want to experience. Allow yourself to feel as though it is already occurring and get swept away in how good it feels. I recommend you stray from writing down specific "things" you desire, and instead record experiences and emotions you want to have.

For a printable Gratitude worksheet, please visit the link in Additional Resources at the end of the book.

JOURNALING

WHAT AND WHY

I have always been amazed at how many of my coaching clients come to me terrified of journaling. There are typically three major blocks for them:

1. They don't know what to write, or how to begin;
2. They feel silly writing out their deep inner thoughts and worry someone will find their journal and read it and laugh at them;
3. They are terrified of what they'll learn about themselves.

The third one always hits me right in the heart. So many of us are walking around in complete delusion about who we truly are . . . and we know it. We would much rather play pretend than face the Truth of who we are, perceived flaws and all. One of the first practices I ALWAYS recommend to clients is to begin daily journaling. It can be one of the most profound tools to self-discovery and exploration. In case you subscribe to any of the three above beliefs, here are my suggestions for you:

- There is no right or wrong way to journal, ever. You actually cannot do it wrong (unless you're not writing anything at all). So use some of the journaling prompts listed below and just start.

- If you feel your journal is unsafe in your home, consider keeping one in your car or at work or somewhere else you feel it's safe. You may also choose to rip out the pages each week and burn or shred them. Journaling isn't about going back to read your words again, it's about getting thoughts out of your head and onto paper.

- Discovering things about yourself is why you're here. Take a deep breath, trust that you will never be dealt more than you can handle, and start writing (and if it's still too much, hire a coach to support you with what truths arise along the way).

WHEN TO USE THIS TECHNIQUE
Daily. When you first wake up. After yoga or meditation. After using the Energy-Release Technique. Before bed. During a full or new moon ceremony.

THE PRACTICE
One of my favorite ways to journal is to ask a question, pause, wait for my hand to feel guided to an answer, and then write the answer. This ritual is me consulting with my Higher Self or with my angels and guides, or sometimes, with my own mind. It's a very fluid, intuitive practice that requires a bit of surrender and openness to whatever thoughts want to be written down.

Another way to journal is to simply recount your day. Some of my clients journal each night on three things they are proud of that day and three things they would like to change for the future. As I mentioned before, there is no right or wrong way to journal except to not write anything at all. Try your best to not get hung up on the "how," and instead just get to writing.

Here are a handful of journaling prompts to help get you started or take your journaling deeper:

- If I were given $1 million today, what would I change about my life?
- If money was not a thing, if I didn't need to earn money or already had more than enough, what would I choose to do with my life?
- What/Who is God to me?
- I feel most feminine/confident/expressed/loved/other when I am . . .
- The legacy I want to leave to my children is . . .
- My ideal morning looks like . . .
- If I could spend a day with my thirteen-year-old self, I'd tell her these three things:
- I am most proud of myself for/because . . .

MIRACLE MINDSET

WHAT AND WHY
Miracle mindset is activating the power of choice in every moment. It's about expecting good things to occur and celebrating when they do. It's noticing when you are feeling frustrated, stagnant, stuck, or agitated, and choosing a different thought, choosing to see the miracle that is possible within that emotion or moment.

This simple and profound technique teaches you to shift yourself from a negative sense of self to a mindset of possibility, prosperity, and love. It can be used in every situation that the material world presents you with to assist you to returning to love. The miracle mindset is where you are aligned with the creative energy of the Universe and all that you need simply flows to you with ease and grace, serving your personal evolution and, in turn, the evolution of humanity.

WHEN TO USE THIS TECHNIQUE
Use this mindset tool all day, every day. It is excellent at helping you stay in a high vibrational energetic frequency, and it feels good to bring yourself to a smile all day.

THE PRACTICE
   Step 1 ~ Identify that you are in a low vibrational thought/emotion.

   Step 2 ~ Physically move your body to release the energetic attachment to the previous thought/emotion (shake your head, shake your wrists, shake your booty).

Step 3 ~ Ask yourself what you want to feel instead.

Step 4 ~ State your new desired thought/emotion over and over again until you can't help but smile and feel full of the magic and miracles of this beautiful world.

SPIRITUAL AWAKENINGS

EARTHING

WHAT AND WHY

Earthing is something that I have done my entire life without knowing this term. It is cultivating a sense of grounding and connection with the natural rhythms of the earth. The earth emits electrical energetic frequencies, just as we do as human beings. When we spend time in nature, our frequency begins to align with and connect to the powerful frequency of the earth.

WHEN TO USE THIS TECHNIQUE

Every day! As much as possible. Of course, if you're like me and live somewhere with snow for months of the year, skin to earth can be quite difficult. However, once you start practicing this technique, simply being in nature will be enough for you to feel her energetic pulse.

THE PRACTICE

There is no right or wrong way to practice earthing; it can become your own personal practice that serves your body. Ideally, you will have direct skin contact with the earth—perhaps you're barefoot in the grass or sitting cross-legged on the sand at the beach. You can be standing, sitting, lying down, or walking with nature for earthing to occur. One of my favorite ways is to place my hands and third eye (center of forehead) on the bark of a tree.

Bring your awareness to your breath as you slow down your thoughts and enter into a meditative state of energetic awareness. Begin to observe what energy you can feel around you and in you. Can you feel the pulse of the plants around you? Can you feel the energetic heartbeat of the earth? Rest here until you feel elevated, awakened, and ALIVE! Thank the earth for sharing her beautiful energy with you and carry on about your day.

PERSONAL CEREMONY

WHAT AND WHY

Ceremony is a beautiful way to physically and energetically make a commitment to yourself and reconnect to your soul's guidance. Often in life we get so caught up in the *doing*. Hosting a ceremony for ourselves (and others) helps to reanchor us with our *being*.

WHEN TO USE THIS TECHNIQUE

Ceremony is often used to open a retreat or sacred space during full and new moons or during a big energetic or life transition. It can also be used to recenter your energetic focus. I've recommended to clients to host a personal ceremony when they are feeling overwhelmed in their masculine energy and are craving a deeper commitment to their spiritual practices. Use your ceremony as a symbol of connection to yourself, your higher self (soul), and to the Universe/God.

THE PRACTICE

Your personal ceremony is meant to be an expression of what feels authentic and true for you. There is no *correct* way to host a ceremony. Follow your intuition and allow it to guide you to what feels right. You may desire to study and explore ancient traditions and cultures to learn more about which traditions feel aligned with your heart. You may feel drawn to light a candle to symbolize your ceremony. Perhaps you will light incense, burn sage, surround yourself with crystals, pull cards, listen to meditation music, dance and chant. A ceremony can be for any length of time that feels nourishing to you. I recommend you give yourself an hour of silence and solitude from your daily commitments to fully surrender into the experience. If you feel complete before the hour is up, beautiful. If you desire to continue longer than an hour, amazing! Let this be *your* personal experience of ceremony!

MEDITATION

WHAT AND WHY

Meditation is an incredible tool to quiet the mind and allow the natural flow of soul wisdom and intuition to be heard/seen/felt. There is no right or wrong way to meditate. Some ancient traditions and philosophies will suggest that you are not to move doing meditation, while others suggest taking any intuitive movement your body is craving. Every person has a different experience, and while there are many different styles of meditation, each experience is unique to the individual person and the individual day. Allow yourself to have your own experience of meditation instead of seeking to *do it right*.

Here I share with you three simple types of meditation to get you started on your own personal practice. Each of these meditations can be downloaded as an audio using the link in the Additional Resources section of this book. Remember, you can't do meditation incorrectly, so release that pressure, get comfortable, and allow your mental chatter to soften as you open to your Truth.

SENSORY AWARENESS

WHEN TO USE THIS TECHNIQUE

Sensory awareness can be used at any time. It is most effective for grounding you into the present moment when you notice you are spinning out in cognitive thoughts in your mind. It helps to anchor you into the space and place you are in now, in this present moment. Use this meditation when you are feeling overwhelmed, stressed, and overly excited.

THE PRACTICE

Begin in a comfortable seated position with your spine long and tall, or lying flat on your back. Rest your hands comfortably in your lap or beside or on your body. Close your eyes and bring your awareness inside your physical body. Notice that your awareness comes away from your thoughts. Allow this drifting to happen. Notice your natural breath: the length of the inhale, a gentle pause at the top, and the length of the exhale. Bring your awareness into your heart and set an intention, your Sankalpa, for your meditation practice.

As you tune into your senses in this present moment, notice the temperature in the room. Notice the warmth or coolness you feel on your skin. Observe how this temperature feels on your body. Notice how comfortable your body feels in this temperature.

Notice three sounds around you. Notice the loudest sound you hear to the faintest one you perceive. Observe these sounds as they enter your ear canal. Notice how comfortable your body feels receiving these sounds.

Bring your awareness into your mouth. What sensations are present in your mouth? What flavor can you taste on your tongue? What sensations can you feel on your bottom teeth, your top teeth, all teeth? Notice the sensation of your top lip and bottom lip pressed gently together. Notice all the sensations in your entire mouth.

Observe the sensation of clothing on your skin. What does it feel like to notice clothing touching your skin? Where on your body is clothing touching you? Notice how familiar this sensation of clothing touching your skin is. Notice how comfortable your skin feels with this clothing touching it.

Notice the carpet, or blanket, or cushion underneath your body. Notice how supported your body is. Notice how easeful your body feels resting and being supported. Allow your body to fully surrender into this rest and support. Allow your body to soften fully into the support beneath you. Allow your body to surrender now.

Begin to bring your awareness back to your breath: notice the length of your inhale, the gentle pause at the top, and the length of your exhale. You are in your body. It feels safe to be in your body. Bring your hands to your heart and say a prayer of gratitude for your mediation practice.

Gently flutter your eyes open and take a moment to give thanks for all objects and beings around you. Take a deep long breath in through your nose, then open your mouth and sigh out.

INTERNAL EXPANSION

WHEN TO USE THIS TECHNIQUE

This internal expansion can be used at any time, for any reason. Allow yourself to use it when you feel intuitively guided to do so. This style of meditation is powerful to use when you feel contractive and scared. It will allow your nervous system to relax and help release you from a *flight or fight* response.

THE PRACTICE

Begin in a comfortable seated position with your spine long and tall, or lying flat on your back. Rest your hands comfortably in your lap or beside or on your body. Close your eyes and bring your awareness inside your physical body. Notice that your awareness comes away from your thoughts. Allow this drifting to happen. Notice your natural breath: the length of the inhale, a gentle pause at the top, and the length of the exhale. Bring your awareness into your heart and set an intention, your Sankalpa, for your meditation practice.

Notice your breath. Notice the sensation of your inhale coming through your nose, reaching all the way into your lungs, and gently releasing through your nose. Notice this natural, easy rhythm of breath. Inhale with ease. Exhale with ease. Inhale with ease. Exhale with ease.

Notice your breath lengthening, reaching all the way to the bottoms of your lungs. Your entire lungs are filling with fresh prana with every inhale. Feel your rib cage expand with every inhale as your lungs fill with air. Observe the gentle inner expansion of your diaphragm creating space for your inhale.

Notice your long easy exhale releasing all air from your lungs. Observe your rib cage gently contract as you exhale all air from your lungs. It feels safe to release all air from your lungs.

Notice your inhale reach to the backs of your lungs. Your breath reaches so deep that you can feel your rib cage expand into the cushion or floor beneath you. Your whole body expands with your inhale, opening, expanding, creating space. Every cell in your body is filling with prana, with life-force energy, with vitality.

Your body is at peace here. Your body is at ease here. This breath feels easy and nourishing to your body. You allow yourself to sink deeper into this breath. Your body is being breathed by your long easy breath. Your body is being breathed by your breath. Your body is at peace. Your body is at ease. You are at peace. You are at ease.

Bring your hands to your heart and say a prayer of gratitude for your mediation practice. Gently flutter your eyes open and take a moment to give thanks for all objects and beings around you. Take a deep long breath in through your nose, then open your mouth and sigh out.

VISUALIZATION

WHEN TO USE THIS TECHNIQUE

This meditation technique is a powerful way to begin your day, reconnecting to your soul-essence and embodying your Truth that you are a vessel of light and love energy. It is also powerful to use when you feel disconnected from your life purpose, your relationships, the Universe, and the natural rhythms of life.

THE PRACTICE

Begin in a comfortable seated position with your spine long and tall, or lying flat on your back. Rest your hands comfortably in your lap or beside or on your body. Close your eyes and bring your awareness inside your physical body. Notice that your awareness comes away from your thoughts. Allow this drifting to happen. Notice your natural breath: the length of the inhale, a gentle pause at the top, and the length of the exhale. Bring your awareness into your heart and set an intention, your Sankalpa, for your meditation practice.

Bring your awareness to the base of your spine: your root chakra. Notice what sensation is present here. Observe the sensation of focusing on your root chakra. What colors or feelings or sensations are present, if any?

Notice an intricate system of tree roots beginning to sprout from the base of your spine. Notice these roots anchor all the way down, down, down through to the core of the Earth. Your root system is now fully connected with the core of the Earth. Feel the vibrancy and potency of energy flowing between the core of the Earth and your root chakra. Notice your whole body being fueled with vitality and energy and creation energy.

Witness this energy begin to swirl its way up your spine—slowly, slowly swirling up around your spine. Notice this vitality swirl around your spine and activate your sacral chakra: your solar plexus and your heart. Notice the energy from the core of the Earth swirling up your spine and activating your throat chakra, your third eye, and the top of your head—your crown chakra. Notice your entire body, your whole being, filled with this vitality and energy from the core of the Earth.

Notice any sensation present at your crown chakra and perhaps even an inch or two above the top of your head. What sensation is present here? What colors or feelings or sensations are present, if any?

Observe a stream of golden healing light begin to pour into your crown chakra from the Universe above. Your whole crown chakra is being illuminated by this golden healing life-force energy. Your body openly receives this healing energy.

Notice this golden healing light pour down through your crown chakra, all the way down through your central column of light, your entire spine, and all your chakras. They are all illuminated by this light. Your entire being is illuminated by the light of the Universe. You are a vessel for the light of the Universe.

Observe the duality of being deeply grounded and anchored into the core of the Earth and being fully illuminated with the healing golden light of the Universe. You are a vessel for light and love. You are the vessel of light and love. You are light. You are love. You are all.

Take a deep breath and bring your awareness into your heart center. Place both your hands on your heart and say a prayer of gratitude for your mediation practice. Gently flutter your eyes open and take a moment to give thanks for all objects and beings around you. Take a deep long breath in through your nose, then open your mouth and sigh out.

INTUITIVE JOURNALING

WHAT AND WHY

Intuitively journaling is different from traditional journaling in that you aren't seeking a specific solution or writing about any one topic. It is an opportunity for your mind to be occupied with the writing aspect, and your intuition and Higher Self are welcome to fully express themselves through your words. It can be a very powerful practice for uncovering intuitive solutions and hidden fears that are blocking your desires.

WHEN TO USE THIS TECHNIQUE

This journaling is a powerful morning practice to use before our minds are influenced and triggered by social media, work, or even our families. I love to intuitively journal while sipping tea in the morning. It's also very useful when you're struggling with a problem and can't find a solution that feels aligned. Coming into an intuitive state of expression can help that solution present itself organically.

THE PRACTICE

Set the timer on your phone (start with three to five minutes and work up to twenty to thirty minutes), use one of the breath techniques shared in this book, choose a topic, then simply begin writing. There is no thought involved, just fluid and intuitive writing on paper. Whatever comes into your mind, write it down. You can change your topic of writing as many times as you like, allowing your mind to express all thoughts, fears, worries, beliefs, desires, etc. on that one topic.

"Whatever your heart is craving, know that you can do it. You wouldn't have the impulse if you didn't already have the goods to make it happen."

~Marie Forleo,
Everything Is Figureoutable

ADDITIONAL RESOURCES

There are a million resources that I wanted to share with you to support your journey home to your Feminine Warrior. But there are only so many pages.

When you are ready to take some of these teachings and principles and resources deeper, I invite you to visit the digital library I have created for you. You will find audio, video, and worksheet downloads to assist you in using your Embodiment tools as well as invitations to coaching programs and unique offerings designed to awaken your soul's true potential. As you enter your digital library, trust your intuition is guiding you to exactly what you need, when you need it. If you feel drawn to one particular tool or resource, follow that inner impulse and observe the magic that ensues.

To access your exclusive additional resources, please visit: www.deannadeacon.com/femininewarrior-resources

CONCLUSION

It isn't enough to want to change; change requires diligent daily commitment and dedication to the expansion of your soul and heart. Every day you need to recommit to your Truth. Allow your focus to see through the eyes of love, instead of returning to the drama of fear. You *have* all that you need, and you *are* all that you need. Trust yourself to take the right steps, at the right time, and know that there will be times when the path feels overgrown, uncertain, and scary. These are the moments to anchor more deeply, to remind yourself of your resilience and strength, and trust in your track record—you've made it through one hundred percent of the heartbreaking moments and seasons in your life thus far.

You are destined for a greatness beyond what your Ego and fear can even fathom. Let yourself dream, let yourself play, let yourself expand beyond your personality, your physical body, and your past. No one person, place, or experience has the power to take your strength.

YOU are the creator of your destiny, a co-creator with the magic of the Universe. And in this moment, remember that anything and everything you desire is completely possible.

I believe in you, Goddess.
I believe in your strength, your compassion, your heart, and your soul.
I see you in your light—your essence illuminating the world around you.
I see your love, your natural easy love, touching the hearts of others every day.
I see you in your brilliance, your magnificence, your Truth.
Now is your time to see yourself clearly.
Choose love.
Choose peace.
Choose joy, over and over again.
And witness your world transform as you live, breathe, and exist as the feminine warrior you have always been.
xoxo

    Deanna Deacon, your coach, mentor, and sister

END NOTES

Page 12

The Dalai Lama, Vancouver Peace Summit 2009

Page 13

Campbell, Rebecca. *Rise Sister Rise: A Guide to Unleashing the Wise, Wild Woman Within.* Hay House UK, 2016.

Page 31

Forleo, Marie. *Everything Is Figureoutable.* Portfolio/Penguin, 2019.

Page 47

Bernstein, Gabrielle. *Judgment Detox: Release the Beliefs That Hold You Back from Living a Better Life.* Gallery Books, 2018.

Page 63

Bernstein, Gabrielle. *The Universe Has Your Back: Transform Your Fear to Faith.* Hay House Inc., 2016.

Page 70

1. How Many Ads Do You See in One Day? (n.d.). Retrieved August 31, 2020, from https://www.redcrowmarketing.com/2015/09/10/many-ads-see-one-day/

Page 71

2. List of women CEOs of Fortune 500 companies. (2020, August 12). Retrieved August 31, 2020, from https://en.m.wikipedia.org/wiki/List_of_women_CEOs_of_Fortune_500_companies

Page 109

Campbell, Rebecca. *Light Is the New Black: A Guide to Answering Your Soul's Callings and Working Your Light.* Hay House Inc., 2015

Page 139

Williamson, Marianne. *A Return to Love: Reflections on the Principles of "A Course in Miracles".* HarperOne, 1996.

Page 164

Hay, Louise L. *You Can Heal Your Life*. Hay House Inc., 1984.

Page 167

Hay, Louise L. *You Can Heal Your Life*. Hay House Inc., 1984.

Page 179

Beckwith, Michael Bernard. *Spiritual Liberation: Fulfilling Your Soul's Potential*. Atria Books/Beyond Words, 2009.

Page 184

Chopra, Deepak. *The Seven Spiritual Laws of Success: A Practical Guide to the Fulfillment of Your Dreams*. ReadHowYouWant, 2009.

Page 189

Maya Angelou quote: https://www.goodreads.com/quotes/5934-i-ve-learned-that-people-will-forget-what-you-said-people, retrieved October 10, 2020.

Page 191

Bernstein, Gabrielle. *Super Attractor: Methods for Manifesting a Life beyond Your Wildest Dreams*. Hay House Inc., 2019.

Page 210

Williamson, Marianne. *A Return to Love: Reflections on the Principles of "A Course in Miracles"*. HarperOne, 1996.

Page 218

Hay, Louise L. *You Can Heal Your Life*. Hay House Inc., 1984.

Page 250

Image created by Vanessa Ooms, Straight Arrow Design.

Page 251

Lynch, Margaret M. *Tapping into Wealth: How Emotional Freedom Techniques (EFT) Can Help You Clear the Path to Making More Money*. Tarcher/Penguin, 2013.

Page 281

Forleo, Marie. *Everything Is Figureoutable*. Portfolio/Penguin, 2019.

ACKNOWLEDGEMENTS

I've dreamt of this moment for years, standing on the metaphorical stage of life and giving my thank-you speech with acknowledgements to all who helped me along my journey. Even at the ripe young age of twelve years old I dreamt of this moment, with sass in my voice, thanking those who've hurt me in the past while smiling from my podium of success. I would stand with pride and spit daggers at those who tried to keep me small, keep me silent, keep me still.

And here I am today, choosing to do the same, except this time there are no daggers, just love. All love. Only love.

To those who bullied me, thank you.
To those who lied to me, thank you.
To those who cheated on me, thank you.
To those who fired me, thank you.
To those who said no to me, thank you.
To those who left me, thank you.

To those who loved me, thank you.

To those who supported me, thank you.

To those who saw me, thank you.

To those who believed in me, thank you.

Each and every one of you have made me into the woman I am today; a woman proud of who she is choosing to be every single day.

Thank you to my family; you have always supported me, even when you didn't know what that meant. You allowed me to find myself, to come home to me.

Thank you to my husband; you are my rock, my anchor, my grounding, always allowing me to fly. You and me together, we can do anything, baby. I love you.

EMBODY YOUR EMPOWERED SELF

in the

Feminine Warrior's Way

LIVE intuitive coaching
and transformational conversations
with Author and Coach Deanna Deacon

www.deannadeacon.com/femininewarriorsway

Are you seeking an intimate community of soul seekers like yourself to do the deep inner work as a community?

Are you committed to creating real TRANSFORMATION in your life, instead of just thinking about it?

Would you like to walk into all situations in life and deeply, truly, TRUST yourself?

Feminine Warrior's Way is a monthly membership created for women like YOU who desire more purpose, more JOY, more confidence, and more balance in their lives.

We're taking the debut book, FEMININE WARRIOR, and elevating it to a transformational experience with live intuitive coaching, a global community of spirit-seeking women, and deep somatic healing ceremonies for a modern woman like you!

This transformational book club gives you the tools and confidence to have healthier relationships, more confidence in your communication, and unconditional love for your body so you can live aligned with your inner vibrancy, resiliency, and feminine strength.

Join your sisterhood now at:

www.deannadeacon.com/femininewarriorsway

YGTMAMA
MEDIA CO.

HELPING WOMEN BIRTH THEIR BRAIN BABIES

At YGTMama Media Co., we help women bring their visions to life.

Through a collaborative and supportive community, we truly value the idea that it takes a village as we bring your Brain Baby into this world. We are a unique and boutique publisher and professional branding company that caters to all stages of business around your book and personal brand as an author. We work with seasoned and emerging authors on solo and collaborative projects.

Our authors have a safe space to grow and diversify themselves within the genres of nonfiction, personal development, spiritual enlightenment, health and wellness, love and relationships, motherhood and business as well as children's books, journals, and personal and professional growth tools. We help motivated women realize dreams and ideas by breathing life into their powerful passions. We believe in women's empowerment, community over competition, and equal opportunity.

JOIN OR CONNECT WITH THE MAMA TEAM

🌐 YGTMAMA.COM

⭕ @YGTMAMA | @YGTMAMA.MEDIA.CO

f @YGTMAMA | @YGTMAMA.MEDIA.CO

Cover Photography by Elisha Isabelle
Cover design by Vanessa Ooms
Development Editor Tania Moraes-Vaz
Edited by Christine Stock
Interior design and typesetting by Doris Chung